T0320096

ALIENATION AND WELLBEING

Chris Yuill

BRISTOL
UNIVERSITY
PRESS

First published in Great Britain in 2024 by

Bristol University Press
University of Bristol
1–9 Old Park Hill
Bristol
BS2 8BB
UK
t: +44 (0)117 374 6645
e: bup-info@bristol.ac.uk

Details of international sales and distribution partners are available at bristoluniversitypress.co.uk

British Library Cataloguing in Publication Data
A catalogue record for this book is available from the British Library

ISBN 978-1-5292-1929-6 hardcover
ISBN 978-1-5292-1930-2 ePub
ISBN 978-1-5292-1931-9 ePdf

The right of Chris Yuill to be identified as author of this work has been asserted by him in accordance with the Copyright, Designs and Patents Act 1988.

Cover design: Liam Roberts Design
Front cover image: iStock/Orbon Alija
Bristol University Press uses environmentally responsible print partners.
Printed and bound in Great Britain by CPI Group (UK) Ltd, Croydon, CR0 4YY

FSC
www.fsc.org
MIX
Paper | Supporting
responsible forestry
FSC® C013604

For Mani, Mansel and Dod.

Life passes too soon.

Glad to have known you and thank you for your insights into life, the beers and the music.

Contents

Acknowledgements

As with everything, this book would not have been possible without Ruth. I thank her for her support and presence in my life. And Harris and Belle, for being Harris and Belle.

I also wish to thank the very much living labour of all the people at Abbotswell Costa, Red Robin, The Cult of Coffee, The Victoria Bar in Torry, Fierce and The Craftsman.

There are so many others to thank too. The people who have participated in various research projects. Everyone who I bumped into along the way at Glastonbury and in Aberdeen Trades Council. I'd also like to thank Norman Stockman in whose class on Sociological Theory I first presented on alienation theory. Bertell Ollman deserves praise too. Thank you for making time to meet with me one lunchtime – I have never learned so much in such a short period of time. In academia, the input of Iain Crinson, Graham Scambler, Iain Ferguson and Michael Lavalette has been invaluable. And to the anonymous reviewer who commented on this project at various stages, I hope I have managed to incorporate your astute and insightful comments.

Preface

George Orwell (1946) always encouraged writers to reveal why they write and why a particular subject interested them: 'I give all this background information because I do not think one can assess a writer's motives without knowing something of his early development. His subject matter will be determined by the age he lives in.' To help assess my motives, and the age I live in, I provide in this Preface an account of what has led me to write this book.

My interest in alienation emerges from two places filled with different sorts of smoke. The first place was the Aberdeen Trades Council and Social Club, the hub of organized labour in Aberdeen until its closure in the 2000s. It possessed a multiplicity of rooms in a grand granite 19th-century building in which various trade unions, community campaigns and political groups held meetings. For some reason most of the meetings I attended were in the badly ventilated at best, windowless at worst, rooms in the basement. It was the 1980s and 1990s, prior to the smoking ban, and a thick acrid fug of cigarette smoke rolled around every meeting. My eyes would be stinging by the end of a speaker's closing remarks. But I learned a lot there. Some of what I learned was to do with the formal part of a meeting and the topics under discussion, such as how to end Apartheid, the General Strike of 1926, gay rights and what this new form of conservative politics called 'neoliberalism' would mean for Britain and working-class people. It was a good grounding in Socialism 101, and a valuable education in theory, politics and history. It was there that I first encountered the thick and lush forest of Marxist theory in which it was so easy to become lost, wandering down the pathways of the forces of production and real subsumption, or ensnared by the thorny bushes of base and superstructure. I remember a young me fumbling through a presentation on alienation in one of those rooms, trying to make sense of concepts such as species-being to both myself and whoever happened to have turned up that night.

But what made the times in those smoky rooms really sing and come alive was the cast of characters who either passed through the rooms on a one-off visit or were regular well-known faces who attended every week. John Londragan was one regular. His life is touched on in the book *Homage to*

Caledonia (Gray 2009) that records the contribution of Scottish volunteers in the Spanish Civil War. An old man at the time, he had served in the International Brigade in Spain fighting fascism in the Civil War. John was one of the Communist Party old guard that seemed to live in the Trades Council building and whose lives had spanned communism from the Russian Revolution in their early childhood to the collapse of the Soviet Union in their senior years. Their passion for politics and protests had never abated though. Whatever the cause at the time they were there. John would burst forth at meetings with his accounts of what it was like to encounter fascism at close quarters and why it needed to be defeated. He punctuated every point he made during meetings with the stab of his right hand, which was minus several fingers courtesy of a fascist bullet during the Battle of Ebro. From him, and the other old Communist Party comrades, I learned something about just how brutal capitalism can be, and what its beneficiaries are happily prepared to do in order to preserve the social relations that maintain their power and privilege. But also, just how hard life was before the National Health Service (NHS) and the welfare state in Britain, and the importance of solidarity and standing by others if you wanted to preserve the gains that his generation had campaigned and fought for.

Jessie was another person I met in the club. She was one of the women who took on the Timex Corporation in Dundee in a bitter, sometimes violent, dispute that lasted for six months in 1993. The Timex Corporation intended to sack workers and cut wages in a factory that had employed people in the city for 47 years. The mainly female workforce decided to fight, to resist the attack by management and save their jobs. She didn't look like a stereotypical revolutionary or agent of change: her hair was bleached blonde and she was dressed, like many other ordinary working-class women at that time, in a bright blue one-piece shell suit. But it was ordinariness that made her and the other women of the Timex strike so powerful.

Various small left-wing political parties were present on the picket lines, but the striking women were fully in charge of the dispute. Chants of "Scabs, scabs, scabs" greeted every bus transporting strike-breakers as they approached the factory gates. The women threw themselves either in front of the bus, or against its sides, bashing at the windows or pointing and naming and shaming the people sitting inside. They were furious with the people in the bus for stealing their jobs and trashing the unspoken codes of community and solidarity that the strikers assumed everyone would stand by and respect. Breaching the codes was unconscionable and an act of class and community betrayal.

"I never thought I could do any of this", said Jessie, as we were coming out of the Unison office at Aberdeen hospital, after doing the rounds of gathering solidarity and strike fund donations. She was referring to how her life had changed during the strike, how she could now stand in front of hundreds of people and talk clearly and confidently, how happy that made her, and for the first time in her life she felt she had meaning and purpose. The change in her life had been achieved not through thinking positively, as recommended in self-help books with their fluffy neoliberal mulch of advocating three sure-fire steps for success, but through being part of a struggle she had learned about herself, that she didn't need to be the person that was quiet and compliant, and do what she was told. Striking can be good for your mental health.

The other place filled with smoke was the Glastonbury Festival of the early 1990s. This time the smoke was wood and weed. Glastonbury was very different then from what it has become in the intervening years. I have written about this period of the festival in *Festival: Before the Rains Came* (Yuill 2018), a fictionalized account of festival life before impenetrable fences, when the people who spent the weekend in tipis were not well-off glampers but people who lived in them the whole year round, moving from festival to festival and wintering somewhere in Wales. More importantly, at that time, the usual powers of control and social discipline were absent throughout most of the festival site. The police were restricted to a very small area around Worthy Farm. I can't remember if this was an arrangement that was negotiated between organizers and the police, or that the police were too apprehensive to venture into what they might have regarded as 'bad lands', haunted by such terrible monsters as new-age travellers, yoga teachers, indie kids and ravers.

It was also a time when politics were very much part of the festival. The Battle of the Beanfield had been fought in England's green and pleasant land just a few years before. A notorious police operation that had targeted new-age travellers which came to a brutal and bloody nadir in June 1985, the Battle of the Beanfield represented everything that was vicious, authoritarian and petty about Thatcherism. A convoy of new-age travellers were forced off the road by the police and into a nearby field. The police then set about the convoy with hammers, smashing the windows of the travellers' vehicles, which also doubled as their homes, and clubbing pregnant women as they tried to escape the police onslaught. John Major's government continued to pursue the authoritarian agenda of Thatcher in the 1990s. It didn't matter if that resistance appeared in the form of the organized working class, the miners and mining communities that had been at the sharp end of deepening ruling class hegemony in 1984, or if the resistance took a cultural form. Firmly in the Tory crosshairs in the early 1990s were the new-age traveller and the raver. Both of which now seem so anodyne and harmless. But they were constructed as folk devils in a convergence of moral panics, as Hall et al (1978) would recognize, that threatened everything from the 'traditional' countryside to the taxes paid by ordinary, decent, hard-working people. The real threat they posed was a rejection of the neoliberal work ethic and living a life that was not built about rampant individualistic consumerism. These folk devils were further attacked with the Criminal Justice and Public Order Act (1994). A piece of legislation that for the first time outlawed a musical time signature (repetitive beats) with the intent of curbing, if not ending, a whole youth subculture. And because Glastonbury at that time was a gathering place at the end of June for travellers, ravers and others it became a site of resistance.

Glastonbury is a vast site, much more than the music stages that are broadcast on the BBC every year when it's on. The music is actually just one element of an array of arts and pursuits. You can find theatre, experimental circus, comedy, alternative healing, alternative energy and anything else you can attach 'alternative' to, and just general out-there stuff you never thought was possible. In the early 1990s a walk into the Green Fields took you into a patchwork of experiences that I had never encountered before.

The Green Fields were a twist of ancient lanes, a disused railway embankment, mature copses and several fields that gave rise to planned and unplanned events that didn't feature in the official programme. And in those fields a spontaneous order seemed to exist. The police were absent, no hi-vis security, just people left to their own devices. Everything seemed to manage by itself. And by the way, it was not a middle-class *Guardian* reader's alternative Butlin's (well, not then at least) that it appears to be now. A wide range of people from different class backgrounds were regular attenders. I remember tradesmen from Liverpool forming a significant demographic, and when the Happy Mondays played in 1990, it felt like half of Manchester's youth had collectively jumped the vague gesture of the perimeter fence.

It was there, as comedian Rob Newman commented, that you could glimpse another world being possible. It was hazy, out-of-focus and ill-defined, and I am stressing the 'glimpsed' part of glimpsing that another world was possible. It would be naive and incorrect to say a whole new form of society was in embryo there. The radical journalist of the time, C.J. Stone, in *Fierce Dancing* (1996), skewers the festival as capitalism in the mud. Everywhere he went he encountered people trying to flog hash, lager or wellies. And not everyone was loved up. There was violence. A nihilist bunch of travellers in 1990 called the Brew Crew, fuelled on industrial-grade cider and Special Brew (hence the name), beat people up and trashed equipment near the field in which they were camped. Close up they were not romantic revolutionaries or free spirits but pissed idiots who were parasitic on traveller culture and other progressive projects. They took Lydon's injunction to get pissed and destroy in the wrong direction, directing their rage against their own side. Other examples of violence may well have occurred but I did not witness them.

Looking back on the early 1990s, I was experiencing a reaction against what Mark Fisher (2009) was to later term capitalist realism. Fisher chronicled, before his untimely death, a period in British history when trying to forge some form of rebellion or resistance seemed impossible. The very *idea* of trying to create a society beyond the capitalist horizon, beyond the logics of neoliberalism and beyond what we have now, he argued, has been all but erased. That is capitalist realism. It is all that there is, Thatcher's dictum of 'There Is No Alternative' has won the day and the wage relation is everything. All that is left, especially for younger people, is a life of hedonic depression and privatized stress. His later writings were concerned with how we burst the illusions of capitalist realism. Fisher saw in what Cowie (2012) wrote about America, as it went from the optimism and rebellion of the 1960s and into the splintered 1970s[1] with the emergence of neoliberalism, the importance of popular culture alongside the discipline of workplace organization, all power to the imagination plus regular activist meetings, as how to gain ground in the class struggle. We need what he called an 'acid consciousness' that could see through the confines of capitalist realism. He was not (necessarily) advocating dropping acid or taking pills, but seeking out places and experiences that allowed a critique of capitalism realism to develop and ideas for a better society to germinate.

Glastonbury, for me, in that period of its history, provided a glimpse of another world. And before anyone thinks I am advocating that a post-alienation society will be a tie-dyed hippy-fest, I am not. All I am saying here is that it provided a little space in which to think differently about how people can relate together, form solidarities and to fire imaginations about how society could be different.

What does all this trawling through the past add to what I am doing in this book? I feel it helps to set the groundwork for the interpretation of alienation presented in the rest of this book. My basic interpretation is that people are wonderful, fantastic and creative beings regardless of where they are positioned in a class society and are capable of more than they believe and are permitted to be by a contradictory society that offers the route of self and collective realization, joy, but then snatches that away through entirely human-made social and economic relations that make our lives a great deal less than they should be. It is in the health and wellbeing, the physical, emotional and mental elements of human existence, that alienation becomes visible and evident. Alienation is about pain, it is about suffering

---

[1]   For a visual account of this transitionary period, the interregnum between the idealism of the 1960s and the splintered 1970s, see street photographer John Duncan's (2021) book on working-class life in Portland. He documents how the deep changes brought by the neoliberalization of the US economy reworked the streets and the lives of people at that time.

and about lives being less than they could, and if I am to moralize for a second, *should* be.

In the forthcoming chapters I take you through how I understand alienation. Much of it is based in Marx, but multiple perspectives from medical sociology (my subdiscipline of sociology) are present too, alongside discussions and debates with contemporary theories. For example, I draw on the expanding literature on neo-materialism that asks questions about agency and its sole location in the activities of humans, and I also engage a little with current Spinozist concerns of affects in the workplace.

Ultimately, I offer suggestions on how we can move from where we are to somewhere better. These suggestions work at different levels from just being nice to other people and recognizing a common solidarity and humanity, to bigger scales of resistance by joining unions, community groups and, perhaps the biggest and trickiest suggestion of all, moving towards some other form of society where social and all other relations between people are set to make us happy and healthy.

Some chapters begin with a vignette, which are summaries of people I've met while undertaking research. I wish to add a human dimension when discussing alienation as discussions of alienation can often be very dry and densely theoretical. By including these vignettes I hope that it takes the study of alienation to that human level but without losing sight of the structures and wider relations which cause alienation. I have also set out to try and write in as open and accessible a style as possible. I agree with Billig (2013) that too much of social science encourages the pursuit of an esoteric writing that values obscuration over clarity. As guitarist Johnny Marr said, "The reason why all those guitar players play so many notes is because they can't find the right one." Whether or not I play the right notes, well, you can judge, though I know at points I do lapse into the safety zone of too much jargon. Thier (2020: 6) makes the similar point that books about Marx 'should only make you cry tears of joy at better understanding the world', rather than tears of frustration at wading through jargon and self-aggrandizing turns of phrase.

1

What Is Alienation?

Jackie's story

Jackie[1] began to cry out of anger. She showed me a picture. It was supposedly the staff room for her and her colleagues to take a break during the day or shelter when it was raining. The room was little more than a small toilet with a microwave on a nearby shelf. The toilet was broken and circled by brown stains on the floor around it. She hated her job. It reduced her to tears most days and she told me about the sense of dread she experienced before she went to sleep and, in the morning, when she awoke about what the day would bring.

Jackie and her co-workers were under pressure to meet ever tighter and more demanding targets. They were traffic wardens working for a private contractor and the targets they needed to meet were handing out as many parking tickets as possible. Boosting the number of tickets meant providing zero leeway for drivers. A second over the allotted parking time and a ticket was issued, even if the driver was approaching and the car park was far from full. Irate rows with drivers were common, adding to the friction of the day. Users of the car park and the traffic wardens became locked into a conflictual relationship, each seeing the other as some form of enemy.

It wasn't the fractious tension with drivers and the shabby working conditions she hated. It was how her job had changed over time. A private contractor had taken over the council's traffic warden operation. When she was employed by the council, she had enjoyed her work. She was not based in a car park but covered the streets in a neighbourhood. There was no pressure to rack up numbers of parking fines issued. She could use her discretion to allow people a few more minutes to move on, or turn a blind eye if she felt that they were having a bad day. Most of her day, in fact, was spent walking around the neighbourhood. She became a known and trusted face to the locals, someone who could be asked to keep an eye on a house if the owners were on holiday, or would say hello and chat to older people if they were on their own.

---

[1]   All names are pseudonyms throughout the book.

1

But when the traffic warden post was outsourced it all changed. She was redeployed immediately to an area that was seen as more revenue-intensive. Her old beat was automated, and her job was replaced by a series of workers on temporary contracts trying to meet daily targets of tickets issued lest their contract was terminated.

Ally's story

"We are not the SAS," said Ally. He was a middle-aged man typical of the oil workers you met when the oil industry defined everything about Aberdeen. He spoke with a strong Doric Scots accent, replete with its own rhythms and words that sharply separate it from other forms of Scots, let alone everyday English, and he was direct and to the point. Ally was also old enough to have been working in 'The Oil' as they say in Aberdeen – and always with the definite article – when the oil rig Piper Alpha, situated 193 kilometres out in the North Sea, was devastated by an explosion in 1988, claiming the lives of 167 of the crew on board.

The disaster led to an upsurge in union activity and the formation of the grassroots trade union, the Offshore Industrial Liaison Committee (OILC). The campaign work and industrial militancy of the OILC resulted in improvements in the conditions for offshore workers, though as Ally was to tell me, the conditions were still pretty grim.

Work for him was the classic pattern of two weeks on and two weeks off on a rig somewhere a hundred miles or so out in the unforgiving North Sea, playing his part in extracting raw petroleum from hundreds of miles beneath the seabed. He was telling me what it was like working out there, the cramped conditions of being in a tight cabin shared with five other men with one toilet between them, long shifts in brutal weather conditions and a way of working that operated to a near military discipline requiring adhering to a myriad of instructions and procedures that made little sense most of the time.

It was the pointless tasks that really got him and his colleagues. The pointless task that irked him the most involved recording health and safety near-misses. It was a regimen that was meant to make work safer but had morphed into a meaningless ritual of collating stats. They were meant to record a set amount of health and safety near-misses every shift. To do so involved a level of creativity. Near-miss reports became works of fiction, with incidents invented or exaggerated. But the fabrication didn't matter, as long as the numbers were created, they could then be placed in a report that seemed to satisfy someone somewhere else in the company.

Ally talked about how a call could come from the employer at any time to get ready to go offshore. That call could come regardless of the time of year. It could come at Christmas, on your birthday, your child or partner's birthday, or at some inopportune time when you were going through a rough patch with your partner and you had to leave without resolving the issue.

That's what he meant by "We are not the SAS" – oil workers, like him, were not emotionless elite soldiers, capable of functioning with no feeling. Despite the hypermasculine image attached to the oil worker, a superhuman sometimes referred to as a 'bear' in local parlance, capable of ignoring storms at sea and able to work in sub-zero temperatures, the industry is populated by people with normal ranges of emotions and fragilities. It hurts missing your kid's birthday, it was tough leaving your partner for two weeks without resolving a row, it was frustrating never being able to plan your life. Ally talked of how all that took an emotional toll on offshore workers that would be manifested in marriage breakdowns, depression and drinking too much, way too much.

Introduction

Jackie and Ally were talking about how their jobs lacked meaning, how they could exert little control over what they did and how it ultimately led to reduced wellbeing and an overall frustration in their lives. Work for them was something that detracted from life. They were tired and exhausted by it. Both reported their wellbeing had suffered and spoke with a level of detachment and despair. They did not like what they saw around them and were sometimes forced into conflict with other people for reasons beyond them. What I will discuss and argue for in this book is that both Jackie and Ally were experiencing alienation, and I mean alienation in the Marxist sense that the relations of capital place demands and restrictions on workers' lives that frustrate, limit and impair health and wellbeing.

Alienation theory promises a great deal in terms of understanding wellbeing. It is a theory that seeks to explain the relationships between wider social and economic relations and human emotions, bodies, desires, potentialities and abilities, between subjective experiences and objective conditions. The alienation theory referred to here is the one developed by Marx. In his writings on capitalism, both in what are referred to as the young and mature Marx, a concern is present with how capitalism damages people, creates social and individual suffering, while limiting the potential and capabilities of people. Linkages in the theory between bodies, labour, production, emotions, minds, brains, and all forms of material things can become visible and allow insights into how and why people suffer, and, moving into normative territory, why that suffering is unnecessary.

It is also timely to consider alienation theory's applicability given the decline of post-modernist theories within medical sociology (Cockerham 2007) and attempts to raise the profile of materialist theories, such as critical realism in (Williams 2003a), and more recently neo-materialism (Fox and Alldred 2016). What the neo-materialist turn, in the broad sense, indicates is that matter matters somehow, and we need to consider how the world in which humans exist is much more than purely discursive or textual as certain post-modernist readings would aver.

Marx though, as Gerhardt (1989) perceptively noted, never developed a discrete theory of health or wellbeing that is laid out as such in an easy to cite chapter or supplementary work. This is not to say that zero mention of health or wellbeing can be found in his writings. Poor health, and the reduced wellbeing of workers, is frequently mentioned as both a normative claim against capitalism and as a point of analysis within the multiple relations of capitalism. In *Capital I* and *III,* for example, Marx provides many examples of how labour affects the health, wellbeing, and bodies and minds of the workers. So, in *Capital I,* Marx (1990: 548) rails against how '[f]actory work exhausts the nervous system to the uttermost, it does away with the many sided play of the muscles, and confiscates every atom of freedom, both in bodily and intellectual activity.' Further, in *Capital III* Marx states:

> The contradictory and antithetical character of the capitalist mode of production leads it to count the squandering of the life and health of the worker, and the depression of his conditions of existence, as itself an economy in the use of constant capital, and hence as a means of raising the rate of profit. (Marx, 1991: 179)

Throughout his writings, and with alienation in particular, a theory of wellbeing can be constructed to analyse and trace the relations that lead to alienation and poor wellbeing. I do not want to engage in a work of Marxology but instead revisit alienation theory, reading it through various theories and innovations that have emerged mainly in medical sociology to put forward why alienation can provide great insight into health inequalities.

Alienation theory and medical sociology

Alienation theory has never received sufficient attention and discussion as a theory in analysing health and wellbeing. Examples of its use to explain the existence of health inequalities, or even health in the workplace, are scant. Glimmers appear in the work of Coburn (1979) and Navarro (1978) on health, but alienation theory has never gained the profile of other theories and concepts within medical sociology. Navarro (1978) was the first contemporary sociologist to argue for a relationship between alienation and poor wellbeing. He clearly tied the extent of psychosomatic conditions experienced by British workers to the loss of control, creativity and self-expression, which he saw as evidence of alienation. While Coburn (1979) found that the more routine and dull work was for workers, the more alienated they became and the worse their wellbeing as a result.

The work of Fromm is also largely absent in the accounts of alienation and health and wellbeing in the sociological literature of this time. Which, again, is a shame, as he does try to bridge the divide between empirical and philosophical approaches to alienation. In *The Sane Society* (Fromm 2002), Fromm sets out his argument with the inclusion of comparative statistics from North America and Europe into his narrative. The point he makes in using statistics that cover alcohol (mis)use, homicide and suicide is that something is deeply wrong in Europe and North America despite other indicators of prosperity that should make for the good life. Fromm's diagnosis of the pathology of modern times is therefore that it is capitalist society that is not sane, that it is in society that the causes of suffering are found.

As with others associated with the Frankfurt School, Fromm draws critically on an eclectic fusion of sources, but mainly Freud and Marx in his case. The thesis he presents in *The Sane Society* centres on human wellbeing situated in a specific society, which possesses certain features that shape the emotional interiority of social beings. He notes that humans in contemporary capitalism inhabit a society that is intrinsically alienating:

> Alienation as we find it in modern society is almost total; it pervades the relationship of man to his work, to the things he consumes, to the state, to his fellow man, and to himself. Man has created a world of man-made things as it never existed before. He has constructed a complicated social machine to administer the technical machine he built. Yet this whole creation of his stands over and above him. He does not feel himself as a creator and centre, but as the servant of Golem, which his hands have built. (Fromm 2002: 121)

The language and tone of this passage are reminiscent of the young Marx. And it is in that humanist tradition that Fromm stands. Modern society, for Fromm, is one where the worker is lost and estranged in a world of corporations and consumerism, where the worker lacks control and is denied 'one's experience of self as the subject and agent of one's powers' (Fromm 2002: 197).

It is in *To Have or to Be?* that Fromm (1979) appraises how consumerist culture damages people. He presents two modes of existence, Being and Having, which affect how social agents act in the world regarding themselves and others. The latter mode refers to not just wanting to own possessions, but to relate to others in a possessive sense too, rather than recognizing and understanding them as of equal value, thus other people become transactional, their value contained only in how they add to status and symbolic advantage. While the former refers to a mode of existence of bringing the interior self into the world through engagement with artistic expression, and engaging in activity for its own sake rather than as part of some status power-play.

The absence of alienation theory within the sociology of health and wellbeing is strange, in many respects, as medical sociology is a field vibrant with theory (Cockerham 2007). In surveying theory within medical sociology, Cockerham and Scambler (2021: 21) proudly exclaimed that 'theory in medical sociology has a rich theoretical tradition spanning almost 60 years and incorporating the work of both classical and contemporary theorists'. They identify the use of a rich and diverse collection of traditions beginning with the structural functionalism of Parsons, and then extending to conflict theories, post-structuralism, post-modernism, feminism, the ideas of Bourdieu or Habermas (1978, 1990) and critical realism. That summary of the field was over a decade ago. Recently, Fox and Alldred (2016) have advocated the application of neo-materialism to the study of health and wellbeing. They draw attention to health and wellbeing emerging out of the micropolitics within assemblages of humans and other matter. Medical sociology thrives on theory and given its theoretical richness it would be reasonable to assume that alienation would have received some attention. Even if that attention was highly critical, the presence of even a negative commentary would be something, but that too is absent.

I suspect that one reason for the lack of alienation theory within medical sociology may be found in the historical development of medical sociology. As a distinct subdiscipline of sociology its genesis begins in the 1980s. At that time, medical sociology as a subdiscipline was finding its own feet and identity, moving away from being bio-medicine's positivist handmaiden, in hock to the medical establishment, to its critic, when it would ally itself with the voices and experiences of patients rather than be directed by the interests and concerns of the medical establishment. The 1980s is significant. It is well after what I have called the 'Golden Age of alienation studies' in the 1960s and the 1970s (Yuill 2011). In the Golden Age of alienation studies, the concept of alienation – albeit not always in a strictly Marxist sense – enjoyed wide popularity. Alienation was the subject of theoretical debate and a sizeable tranche of empirical research. The period was not without its problems. Theorists and empiricists, Marxists and non-Marxists formed opposite and warring camps, but, nevertheless, alienation theory was still highly prominent within sociology. I discuss later why alienation lost its place within the theoretical firmament, but what matters here is that alienation displayed little visibility and usage from the early 1980s onwards. The new theoretical kid on the block was post-structuralism and that *oeuvre* rapidly became dominant (Cockerham and Scambler 2021). Foucault's (2002) archaeology of the clinic providing a powerful stimulus for theoretical development within medical sociology, especially in the United Kingdom. Alienation theory, and Marxism in general, took a back seat from that period onwards within sociology generally and within medical sociology in particular (though with honourable exceptions, such as the aforementioned work of Navarro and Muntaner in the United States).

The Golden Age of Alienation Studies

The Golden Age of alienation studies existed from the turn of the 1960s until the early to mid 1970s: a time of political upheaval and resistance. Across the globe orthodoxies were being challenged. Anti-colonial movements, groups representing oppressed and exploited people, gays, women, people of colour and workers were taking to the street, setting up community groups and occupying workplaces. From Algiers to Vietnam, Detroit to Belfast, it felt as if a tectonic shift was occurring. That a fairer, more equal world could come into being, where old hierarchies and orthodoxies of the past could not just be challenged but *actually* overthrown. Many of the struggles intertwined and inspired each other.

In Algeria the nationalist Front de Libération Nationale began resistance to the French colonial powers in 1954. Algeria had been colonized by the French between 1840 and 1847, and a repressive colonial apparatus had evolved to maintain French domination. French settlers were accorded the same full rights as French citizens while the indigenous population were subjected to the *Code de l'indigénat*, a highly oppressive set of laws that criminalized any act of resistance. The insurgency was met with brutal repression by the French, killing between 150,000 and 300,000 Algerians by the war's end in 1962, when the Algerians won their independence. As Fanon (2001: 29) said of the French authorities, the 'agents of government speak the language of pure force'. The uprising threatened the stability of France itself. The Fourth Republic crashed down, allowing for the rise of right-wing General de Gaulle and the extinguishing of that revolutionary impulse.

The anti-colonial uprising in Algiers rippled into the Paris Uprising of 1968 that came close to a fully-fledged revolution. At its height, workers were in control of major parts of French industry and important services such as power were controlled by workers. Within the demands for better working conditions there were many other demands that stretched beyond a radical reordering of the workplace into how everyday life could be different. 'All power to the imagination' was a popular slogan at the time. It encouraged the thinking, the imagining, of making the world different, going beyond the bounds of what bourgeoisie rigidity offered. The promise of Paris 1968 was never fully realized. The machinations of union bureaucracy, lack of clear revolutionary leadership and the actions of the French state undermined what could have been a significant advance for workers not just in France but across the globe.

That zeitgeist of deep social change in turn influenced academia, leading to the inclusion of areas of study such as feminism. Alienation studies formed part of the radicalism of the times and its popularity as a subject of study was, in many respects, tied into what was happening on the streets and in workplaces. As Musto (2010: 90) has noted of these near-revolutionary times: 'The concept of alienation seemed to express the spirit of the age to perfection.' I have provided a fuller account of this period elsewhere (Yuill 2011),[2] but I will provide a summary of the main points here.

First, contrasts existed in the study of alienation either side of the Atlantic. Two paintings illustrate the differences between Europe and the United States. Hopper's *Nighthawks* painting provides a visual metaphor of alienation studies in the United States. In that classic work three people appear disconnected and alone in a late-night urban diner. The worker, the male and female customers are presented on the same level, all equally experiencing displacement and alienation from each other. In Europe it is Manet's *Un Bar aux Folies-Bergère*. Centre is the worker, in this case a young woman. She is depicted as much as an object on display and as commodified as the champagne and the bottle of Bass beer in the fore of the painting. It is her eyes, her blank stare, that signals alienation. She tries to affect a neutral expression suppressing sadness and despondency. The figure of a man, the capitalist engaging in the process of alienation, dominating the existence of the woman worker, also lurks in the painting.

The American literature, especially the empirical literature, tended to focus on the psychological experiences of alienation, drawing on an eclectic source of perspectives. Seeman (1959) played a central role in American alienation studies. His explicitly descriptive approach and social-psychological rendering of alienation was an attempt to make the philosophical concept of alienation operational as a research problematic. The theory Seeman drew from was diverse and eclectic, drawing from Durkheimian anomie, Mannheimian functionalism and substantial rationality, in addition to Marxian notions of *Entfremdung*. In his schema of alienation, Seeman (1959) identified six varieties and expressions that alienation could take: powerlessness; meaninglessness; normlessness; cultural estrangement; self-estrangement; and social isolation. The European material, meanwhile, focuses on the sociological causes of alienation, drawing on differing readings of Marx. Its concern was more on the exploitation of workers and the revolutionary potential, or otherwise, of the working class. The European wing of alienation studies was far from harmonious. The humanist Marxism of Lefebvre (1968, 2004, 2014) and Lukács (1975) and the anti-humanist structural Marxism of Althusser (1969) were at odds with each other as to how to interpret Marx: especially whether or not Marx had dropped alienation theory from his overall analysis as he matured (a fraught debate rehearsed in Chapter 2).

---

[2] Hands up, this account is far too Eurocentric and omits insights from scholars such as Fanon. I try to address that flaw here, while realizing that much more needs to be done.

The radical humanism of Fanon (2021a) is omitted from discussions of alienation theory in the 1960s and 1970s. His work adds a much-needed dimension to understanding alienation. All of the material discussed here originates from the Global North. Capitalism, and its colonial projects, are experienced globally, but the theorization and empirical work in the past was focused on Europe and North America. Fanon brings insights into how particular historical circumstances create specific experiences of alienation, and with it an innovative, creative but always questioning engagement with Marxism that critically probed the relevance of Marxism for the anti-colonial struggle. Marxism, Fanon (2001: 31) therefore claims, requires 'stretching' and reworking to fully comprehend a time of struggle.[3] As Rabaka (2011) makes clear, Fanon was always critical of European Marxists whose horizons were bounded only by their own continent and who therefore easily slip into become part of what Fanon (2001: 7) referred to as the 'colonial vocabulary', that still seeks to put the needs of Europeans, however exploited, above that of colonized people.

Fanon's focus falls on how under colonialism the identities, cultures and histories are negated by the arrival of colonial powers that seek to dissolve the interiority of colonized racialized people and replace that interior with the norms and cultures of the White colonizer. That estrangement from self and identity, in addition to the brutalization of labour, becomes the experience of alienation, where a profound alienation from self occurs:

> And in the first case [that of the intellectual], alienation is of an almost intellectual character. In so far as he conceives of European culture as a means of stripping himself of his race, he becomes alienated. In the second case [that of the worker], it is a question of a victim of a system based on the exploitation of a given race by another, of the contempt in which a given branch of humanity is held by a form of civilization that pretends to be superiority. (Fanon 2021a: 198)

---

[3] Marx has been criticized for eurocentrism, with some of his analyses sharing the colonialist assumptions common among Europeans of the 19th century. As K.B. Anderson (2016) has argued, the early Marx is guilty as charged but developed a considerably more sophisticated analysis of colonialism and how global history unfolded. He bases his argument on readings of the older Marx's notebooks archived in the Marx-Engels Gesamtausgabe (MEGA) that have not been formally published, but contain a wealth of information on how Marx's thinking was developing. K.B. Anderson (2016: 244) concludes his analysis of this work as follows: 'Marx developed a dialectical theory of social change that was neither unilinear nor exclusively class-based. Just as his theory of social development evolved in a more multilinear direction, so his theory of revolution began over time to concentrate increasingly on the intersectionality of class with ethnicity, race, and nationalism.'

Had Fanon been read more widely by sociologists and others working in alienation studies at the time in Europe and North America, then the field could have been made more vibrant and enlivened by ideas emanating external to Europe that would have solved some of the problems that beset the Golden Age. Tensions between empirical and theoretical wings of alienation studies were a feature of this time, each side claiming that either researching or philosophizing alienation was the only way to approach studying alienation. The lack of communication between the two wings resulted in undertheorized empirical work and philosophy that spoke only to itself, which ultimately restrained and blunted the reach of alienation studies, reducing it to either formulaic research methodologies or impenetrable stultified prose. Fanon, very much in line with how Marx understood the development of theory and of successful struggle, argued that theory and the struggles of people informed each other. Capitalism, and the conflicts endemic to it, produces new struggles, new historical forms of exploitation, and old or received ways of understanding society therefore require constant interrogation and revision. That is what Fanon meant by stretching Marx. The main message, however, from Fanon's work is that race matters. Any theories that occlude race and colonialism do not fully speak to the suffering of the world.

Why did alienation studies lose its place in sociology? The radicalism of the streets and the factories that had fuelled what nearly became a revolution began to fade in the 1970s. While many gains and concessions had been won, a wave of reaction occurred from the mid 1970s onwards. It was the beginning of what was to become known as neoliberalism. The capitalist class wanted to not just wind the clock back on the gains that workers had made, but to further entrench ruling-class power. The offensive took place on a variety of fronts, both theoretical and material, landing like an iron idea wrapped in an iron fist. Pincohet's coup in Chile in 1973 that overthrew the democratically elected Allende government witnessed the imposition of neoliberalism via murdering opponents in football stadia and the bringing in of the Chicago Boys to advise on how the country's economy could be run on neoliberal lines. It portended the world we now live in, in which market freedom is sacrosanct but personal freedoms are eroded and reduced to consumerist horizons. In the United States and the United Kingdom, neoliberalism also arrived in the form of vicious class conflict. The government of Thatcher led an assault on organized labour with its campaign against mine workers and the National Union of Mineworkers, while in the United States Reagan also sought to undermine and weaken labour unions and organized labour.

These defeats for working class and other forms of resistance exerted a toll on the intellectual and theoretical traditions of Marxism. Some in the academy, in particular those who had been enthused by the Paris Uprising of the 1960s, were left, as Žižek (2009) and Bensaïd (2009) both noted, dejected and directionless. The new theories of Foucault and forms of post-modernist thinking became the central concerns of the French intelligentsia, and the ideas of Marx began to fall from favour.

Parallel to changes in the political climate, work was also changing, at least work in the Global North. One commonality of all the Golden Era empirical work was the traditional plant factory. The participants in that research worked on production lines, the classic Fordist subject, an invariably male worker operating in a tightly controlled and monitored regime, as so well recounted and analysed by Braverman (1998). But as the 1980s progressed – at least in the Global North – new forms of work emerged that were disruptive of the old Fordist order. A shift towards the service industries and a feminization of work was occurring. These new forms of work outwardly appeared to be quite different. An ability to work a lathe was replaced by an ability to smile. Marxism seemed no longer capable of charting the new lands of work that were opening up. It appeared lost in time as the new industries operated in the Global North that moved away from extractive or plant industries. New theories emerged with a focus on subjectivity that were supposedly more agile and up to the task of analysing the new workplaces appearing on the industrial landscape.

The final *coup de grâce* for alienation theory as a concept within sociology came with the relocation of the sociology of work (as mentioned before, an obvious home for the study of alienation) away from sociology schools into the new 'business' schools throughout the 1980s and 1990s. Such a migration led – following Strangleman's (2005) observation – to a reduction in the critical reach of the sociology of work to one more in keeping with the theoretically less ambitious disciplinary requirements of 'human resources'. Issues of workplace emotional and physical suffering are now couched in concepts such as 'stress' and 'work–life balance'. As Calnan and Wainwright (2002) note in their critique of the 'work stress epidemic', positing emotional distress in such a way creates a shallow understanding of its causes. Attention is drawn away from critical explorations of the relations between historical and social structures to be replaced by conservative appeals to therapeutic cures and job redesign. The sociology of work is also now less prominent within the curricula of sociology courses, with topics such as globalization, consumerism and the body increasing in profile. Such a development is regrettable even if consumerism has surpassed class and work identities, *pace* Bauman (1998), but engagement in paid and unpaid labour still very much structures and conditions everyday lived experiences.

That is not to deny that problems have existed with how alienation theory has been developed and discussed in the past. To claim that it is perfect and needs only to be rolled out would be nonsense. Alienation theory suffers from what Ricoeur (1968) has referred to as 'semantic overload', where there is so much said about alienation that no one really knows what it is. A similar point was made nearly a decade before Ricoeur, by Clark (1959: 849) when he wrote: 'As the list of authors has grown, however, so has the variety of definitions of the concept or fractions of it.' Indeed, one criticism of alienation theory is that while it is superficially attractive, perhaps even intuitively correct, with its talk of suffering, when you try to get a hold of alienation it disappears amid an array of concepts that are difficult to flesh out or apply empirically. Reflecting on the Golden Age material, the observation can be also made that much of the empirical work lacked nuance and presented a clumsy ham-fisted approach to researching alienation (Archibald 1978; Yuill 2017). The fluid dialectical relationship between theory and findings that is the hallmark of a Marxist approach was absent in that material. Instead, a reductive positivism formed the main research agenda, which created drawbacks with what the research revealed. And then there are the perennial charges and criticisms of essentialism, paternalism, denigrating nature, totalizing everyday life and forgetting to take account of human agency. All of that and not forgetting Althusser's claims of an epistemological break in Marx. Althusser's (in)famous wager was that the mature Marx rejected his youthful dalliance with humanism, alienation in particular, and progressed to developing a scientific problematic of structure over humanist subjectivity and reference to human nature.

Whatever the reasons for alienation theory's current lack of profile within medical sociology – and perhaps sociology more widely – this book lays out a rationale for including alienation within the toolkit of theories that explain why the societies in which social agents live result in so much suffering, evident in poor health and wellbeing. In the remainder of this chapter, I outline what Marx said about alienation. And in Chapter 2 I return to and tackle the criticisms and charges I mentioned earlier.

What is alienation?

Marx was not the first to theorize alienation. A history of alienation writing before Marx stretches from the Enlightenment-era philosophy of Rousseau (1754, 1762), to the conservative Romanticism of Carlyle (1829) and Ruskin (2012) to the proto-sociology of Fergusson (Brewer 1989, 2007; Hill 2007). Then, of course, there is Hegel, whose ideas on alienation will be encountered and discussed later. The one unifying observation that can be made about this pre-Marxian history of alienation is that it tends to be idealistic in nature, usually nostalgic and Lapsarian in content, all of which is quite different from how Marx understood alienation.

In this section the basics, an Alienation 101, is laid out and summarizes the main features of what Marx wrote about alienation. It provides a reminder of what Marx said and then lays the basis for more in-depth discussion of many of the criticisms of alienation theory that have emerged over time. If you feel sufficiently acquainted with alienation theory then please skip ahead to Chapter 2, where issues such as the relationship with nature, essentialism, paternalism, the continuity of alienation within Marx's thought, and other issues, are tackled in greater depth.

Let us begin, as Marx did, with alienation in the *Economic and Philosophic Manuscripts* (EPM from now on). In this early work, which remained unpublished in his lifetime, he engages with alienation most directly, forming a discrete section within the overall work. It is also a point in his philosophical and theoretical development where he is moving away from Hegel and Feuerbach, both of whom provided the initial impetus for his ideas, the rejection and adaptation of whom ultimately leading to the deep critique of capitalism found in his later works. Central to Marx and his thinking at this time was human subjectivity and how human nature is affected by the historical appearance of private property.

In the section of the EPM that specifically deals with alienation, *Estranged Labour*, Marx begins with a critique of political economy, and its elision of the exploitation and alienation of the worker, and the absence of any explanation of where private property comes from in the first place. It is silent on these issues. What Marx does next is to fill in that gap and provide an answer to these questions that political economy leaves in abeyance.

The answer is that capitalism commodifies everything. All is transformed into a commodity. What had been nature, what had been people, now become commodities. All is there to be bought and sold. And the only way for the commodified worker to survive in a capitalist society is to sell themselves in the labour market. As Marx (1977: 63) puts it: 'Labor produces not only commodities; it produces itself and the worker as a commodity.' This arrangement is therefore built not on an equal basis, where two social agents encounter each other as equals, but, instead, it is asymmetric and built on the coercion of the worker.

During the labour process, the worker produces something in the material world, and an objectification of the worker occurs. Unlike Hegel, who saw any objectification in the material as a sign of alienation, Marx does not. Objectification can be good, it can be positive, rewarding and enriching. It can be something where the producer of the object draws some form of realization or positive affect. But under capitalism that relationship between producer and object is destroyed. The object is removed from the worker by the capitalist. The worker is estranged from what they have produced, and it becomes something alien, and this is an act, or in Hegelian terms a moment, of alienation.

13

The following extract is commonly cited in any discussion on alienation. It is where Marx lays out his version of alienation. Within this one paragraph the basic premises of his theory of alienation can be found:

> First, the fact that labor is external to the worker, i.e., it does not belong to his intrinsic nature; that in his work, therefore, he does not affirm himself but denies himself, does not feel content but unhappy, does not develop freely his physical and mental energy but mortifies his body and ruins his mind. The worker therefore only feels himself outside his work, and in his work feels outside himself. He feels at home when he is not working, and when he is working he does not feel at home. His labor is therefore not voluntary, but coerced; it is forced labor. It is therefore not the satisfaction of a need; it is merely a means to satisfy needs external to it. Its alien character emerges clearly in the fact that as soon as no physical or other compulsion exists, labor is shunned like the plague. External labor, labor in which man alienates himself, is a labor of self-sacrifice, of mortification. Lastly, the external character of labor for the worker appears in the fact that it is not his own, but someone else's, that it does not belong to him, that in it he belongs, not to himself, but to another. Just as in religion the spontaneous activity of the human imagination, of the human brain and the human heart, operates on the individual independently of him – that is, operates as an alien, divine or diabolical activity – so is the worker's activity not his spontaneous activity. It belongs to another; it is the loss of his self. (Marx 1977: 65–66)

There is a great deal to work through in this passage. A useful place to begin, given my focus on wellbeing, are the lines relating to what we would now refer to as health and wellbeing: 'he does not feel content but unhappy, does not develop freely his physical and mental energy but mortifies his body and ruins his mind'. That segment is intriguing. Presented here is a clear statement that alienation is evident in the all-round diminishing of health and wellbeing of the individual human. Marx refers to emotional states, physical health and mental health, that the entirety of what it is to holistically possess good health and wellbeing is altered and affected by alienation. Humans are posited as vulnerable beings who are capable of suffering.

Why does this suffering occur, what is it about the society in which social agents exist that leads to the diminishing of their health and wellbeing as we have just seen? The cause, for Marx, can be found in the *historical* form that labour takes in capitalist society:

> He feels at home when he is not working, and when he is working he does not feel at home. His labor is therefore not voluntary, but

coerced; it is forced labor. It is therefore not the satisfaction of a need; it is merely a means to satisfy needs external to it. (Marx 1977: 65–66)

Marx centres that the social organization of work, the objective fact that workers are coerced and forced in their labour, is to blame for suffering. It is not poor decision making by individual social agents, to drink or smoke too much, nor is it the outcome of natural causes, or some random act of bad luck, but the outcome of social and economic relations beyond the agency of individual humans.

The immediate cause of this suffering rests on the loss of control over what is made and how it is made:

[T]he external character of labor for the worker appears in the fact that it is not his own, but someone else's, that it does not belong to him, that in it he belongs, not to himself, but to another. Just as in religion the spontaneous activity of the human imagination, of the human brain and the human heart, operates on the individual independently of him – that is, operates as an alien, divine or diabolical activity – so is the worker's activity not his spontaneous activity. It belongs to another. (Marx 1977: 65–66)

In these lines Marx is sketching out that control constitutes an important element within alienation. The worker has no control both over the labour process and what happens to the object, the commodity, that is produced. They enter into the labour process not as a free agent but as someone coerced or compelled into this activity. Here, the object that is made in the external world is removed by someone else, the capitalist. The object, instead of acting as a vibrant reflection of the creativity, the powers and potentialities of the social agent, is instead removed from the worker and that feeling of realization, the spontaneous activity, is not achieved. The object of production then gains a power over the worker. It becomes an entity that controls the worker. The loss of the object to the capitalist has further implications. Workers cease to relate to other workers as other people: they do not relate to each other as fellow producers but through the objects they produce.

The EPM also outlines other important elements that help to explain alienation. The first is that human beings exist in nature. As Marx worked his way away from Hegel's idealism it took him to a material understanding of humanity, that humans are beings that exist as fleshy, emotional and natural human beings. As Marx (1977: 67) states: 'Man lives on nature – means that nature is his body, with which he must remain in continuous interchange if he is not to die.' This observation might seem quite prosaic. Subtract the basics of life such as food or dwellings, as Marx also refers to in this section of the EPM, and humans perish. But what he posits here is that nature is vital for humanity. Without nature humans are nothing. But Marx notes that humans are not quite the same as other animals. Humans possess a species-being which needs to be distinguished from species-life, a term that Marx also uses. The latter refers to the basic functions of life (the need for nutrition, hydration and so on) but the former refers to an aspect of being human that is much richer and more important. It the capacity or potential of humans to act on nature consciously and cooperatively. It is, for Marx, the definitive point of difference between humans and animals.

The basic run of alienation theory is therefore that human beings find some form of realization and self through their labour, however, under capitalism that cannot happen as their labour is estranged from them, which results in a loss of control over what they make and what happens to the object they make.

Marx (1977) identifies that alienation exists in four different forms, each form relating to aspects of his general philosophy. These four different of modalities of alienation are an attempt by Marx to capture as much as possible of human existence (Ollman 1976). The four expressions encompass the relationship workers have with their product, the relationship workers have with the production process, the relationship that workers have with other humans, and the relationship with human nature. I present them here as separate entities but that is only to make the exposition clearer. In an empirical context they overlap and occur simultaneously or perhaps not at all, but I come back to that when I consider how alienation may exist in everyday life.

Product alienation

Unalienated labour provides humans with a sense of self-realization and affirmation of species-being. The enrichment of self that is found in unalienated labour is reversed in alienated labour where there is instead a 'one-sided enrichment of the object' (Ollman 1976: 144). This inversion occurs because in capitalist society, despite it being the worker who produces objects in their work (whether it is circuit boards on a computer in traditional manufacturing or the smile on a face in the service sector), they do not own that object. Rather the object is owned (or just as powerfully perceived to be controlled) by the capitalist. Importantly for Marx, ownership does not necessarily mean legal ownership but effective ownership of the product. Therefore, the maker of the circuit board may never own the computer for which she constructs parts and the service worker who smiles may perceive her smile as not being her own but as owned by the company for which she works. This results in the object becomes something over which the producer, the worker, has no ownership and therefore considers alien and potentially something that confronts the worker.

Further to that point, under capitalism the object a worker produces can begin to dominate them. The creative power, that vital aspect of humanity's natural disposition, is permanently lost to the worker during the capitalist alienating production process. All that creative power – the energy, thought and consideration that it requires to make something – vanishes into the object of alienated production, which in turn is not replaced by other revitalizing creative power generated by the satisfaction gained by completing a task. Instead, the worker receives only money with which they can purchase other commodities which themselves are the object of someone else's lost, alienated creative power. Therefore, there is no sense of achievement or satisfaction in labour in capitalist society – it is a one-way process of the worker drawing out and giving away sometimes quite deep, life-affirming aspects of self in order to receive no equal or greater creativity in return, or as Marx (1977: 63) states, 'the worker puts his life into the object', with the object retaining that life and stealing it from the worker. This 'putting of life into the object' is especially so for work that requires emotional labour, and this point is elaborated on next.

Hochschild's (1983) work on 'emotional labour' provides a good example of the relationship between a worker's product becoming alien, hostile and something out of their control, and consequent poor health. Hochschild focuses on how the shift towards a service sector economy has led to workers relying not just upon their physical or mental labour but increasingly on their emotional labour. This form of labour is where the workers' actual emotions become 'transmuted' to serve the needs of capital and the particular industry in which they work, the end result being those smiles and expressions of care, for instance, becoming products and the property of the company and not the individual (Hochschild 1983: 198; Hughes 2003: 7). Hochschild (1983: 8) herself notes that for the workers she interviewed, their smiles 'were seen as an extension of the make-up, the uniform, the recorded music, the soothing pastel colors of the airplane décor, and the daytime drinks, which taken together orchestrate the mood of the passengers'. The service sector may not have existed to the same extent in Marx's day when extractive and heavy manufacturing industries were dominant. This change in industry does not, however, mean that the service sector and its particular negative emotional consequences for workers' health are not amenable to a Marxist analysis. One fundamental point that Marx makes about capitalism is that is a constantly revolutionizing system that is always seeking out new frontiers, new markets and new ways of working, thereby becoming unendingly dynamic, assembling and reassembling and melting all fixed and frozen relationships into air to ensure that profit is realized (Berman 1999). It is therefore fundamentally wrong to regard Marx's writings as only relating to heavy industry as he himself recognized that capitalism is in constant reconfiguring flux. So, for Marx, the type of industry is not of prime importance but rather the relationship between people. Callinicos (1989: 127) summarizes this well, when he comments that 'the fact that much of this labour now involves interacting with other people rather than producing goods does not change the social relations involved'.

This situation is exemplified when the air stewardesses in Hochschild's study complain that they no longer feel that their smiles, the welcoming caring emotion that company training demands that they contribute to their work, belong to them but rather to the airline for which they work. The ramifications of emotional labour on wellbeing are quite considerable. As Williams (1998: 754), commenting on Hochschild, observes: '*The Managed Heart*, for example, is replete with references, to the "human costs" of emotional labour, from "burnout" to feeling "phoney", "cynicism" to "emotional deadness", "guilt" to self "blame"'.

Labour process alienation

Allied to the previous point concerning how having no or little control over the object of production can result in alienation, is also the issue of having little control of the actual process of production. As Ollman (1976: 141) suggests, product alienation and process alienation are on a par with each other, both being intimately related to that essential abuse of the creativity of human nature under capitalism. The labour process under capitalism becomes one where the worker – and this can be in a variety of locations (for example, shop worker or academic) as Ferguson and Lavalette (2004) indicate – loses control over workplace organization which has potential negative ramifications for the worker both physically and mentally (Cox 1998). The result is that the worker loses sight of her natural disposition to labour and 'as soon as no physical or other compulsion exists, labour is shunned like the plague' (Marx 1977: 66).

In *Capital I* and *III* Marx provides many examples of how process alienation affects the health, the bodies and the minds, of the workers. So, in *Capital I* Marx (1990: 548) rails against how '[f]actory work exhausts the nervous system to the uttermost, it does away with the many sided play of the muscles, and confiscates every atom of freedom, both in bodily and intellectual activity'. Further, in *Capital III* Marx states:

> The contradictory and antithetical character of the capitalist mode of production leads it to count the squandering of the life and health of the worker, and the depression of his conditions of existence, as itself an economy in the use of constant capital, and hence as a means of raising the rate of profit. (Marx 1991: 179)

There are many other examples where Marx highlights how process alienation and its effect on the bodies and minds of workers result in, as Ollman (1976: 138) summarizes, 'stunted size, bent backs, overdeveloped and underdeveloped muscles, gnarled fingers, enlarged lungs and death pale complexions'. Particularly, there is much invective concerning the treatment of women and children who, for instance, endure 'insufficient nourishment, unsuitable food, and dosing with opiates' (Marx 1990: 521).

An example from the empirical literature that illustrates the effects of process alienation is that of the Whitehall I and Whitehall II studies of Whitehall civil servants (Marmot et al 1997, 1999). Forbes and Wainwright (2001: 810) have commented, but do not develop further, that the evidence and results from the studies appear 'to be directly related to the Marxian concepts of alienation and exploitation'. The research has identified that among civil servants of differing ranks there are decidedly different experiences of health that appear to relate to how much control a worker has in their workplace. In both studies there is a clear social gradient in mortality (Marmot et al 1984) and morbidity (Marmot et al 1991). In these studies we see how a worker's health is affected by the extent of their control (examples include choosing what to do at work, in planning, or in deciding work speed) within their working environment (Bosma et al 1997), and how on a variety of measures the health, whether physical (for men and women) or mental (mainly for men), is influenced by the position or rank that they hold within the organization (Martikainen et al 1999). This chimes very much with the alienation that arises out of the labour process where 'instead of developing the potential inherent in man's powers, capitalist labour consumes these powers without replenishing them, burns them up as if they were a fuel, and leaves the individual worker that much poorer' (Ollman 1976: 137).

Other-human alienation

Other-human alienation takes us away from the 'immediate sphere of workplace relations' (Rees 1998: 90) and into the wider corrosive effects of alienation in its extension into society. Other humans cease to be fellow humans but are transmuted into 'extensions of capitalism' (Ollman 1976: 144), and we are aware of them only by the objects, the commodities they produce – the consequence of commodity fetishism with its obscuring of the social relations that lie behind production. This can lead to seeing others as a source of competition, for example, for better work or more favourable conditions within the workplace (Ollman 1976: 207).

Marx is making the point here that fellow human alienation creates antagonistic divisions between both the worker and the capitalist and between the worker and other workers. This is a society that is rife with division, cutting into that important characteristic of human collectivity, where people encounter fellow humans only as the objects of their production or as superiors or inferiors. Discussion of a society that is divided, or lacking in social cohesion, draws me to the, sometimes rancorous, debate surrounding Wilkinson (1996) and his psychosocial perspective (for a wider Marxist discussion of this work, see Crinson and Yuill 2008).

Human-nature alienation

The first two aspects of alienation – product and labour – are arguably tied in very closely to the actual moments of production, whether in the worker's relationship with the object she produces or in the organization of the work process in which she finds herself. The second two – fellow humans and, under present discussion, human nature – relate to wider social manifestations of alienation. The final aspect of alienation relates to what it is to be human and what separates humans from animals, in that humans have the ability to labour on nature to progress humanity as a whole; this is human's all important defining 'species-nature'. Alienated labour, for Marx, under capital with its relentless pursuit of profit prevents humans from carrying out that fundamental aspect of human existence. As Cox (1998: 51) succinctly puts it, '[w]e have the ability to consciously plan our production, to match what we produce with the needs of society. But under capitalism that ability is reversed by the anarchic drive for profits'.

Taking things forward

For anyone acquainted with the history of Marxist thought the sketch of alienation presented in this chapter could be easily classified (or even dismissed?) as belonging to the humanistic problematic of the early Marx with its focus on human nature. I return to this point in Chapter 2, where I deal with Althusser and his critique of Marx that his early work should be ignored, as it is too steeped in the humanism of Feuerbach to provide a scientific understanding of how capital is structured and, for him, can be ultimately overthrown. As a minor plot spoiler, I do not accept that position and argue a continuity exists between the younger and older Marx, albeit one that is complex and exhibiting change and enrichment. The later works do provide a great deal of insight and elaboration on how alienation in capitalist society can be understood. While alienation may not be so prevalent a concern in *Capital* as it was in the EPM, it is definitely present in *Grundrisse*, where Marx identifies the objective conditions in which alienation occurs. The later works therefore provide insight into the structures of capitalism and flesh out the social structures in which alienation occurs. In other parts of this book, I draw on the later work to further develop how alienation theory can provide insights into wellbeing.

Before finishing this chapter, I want to add something from my own research with social workers. I found that alienation was far from a zero-sum game (Yuill 2018). Definite evidence existed of what I would classify as alienation: many had experienced a 'crash point' where their wellbeing was impaired, resulting in long-term illness, fatigue or disillusionment. But alienation was far from totalizing all aspects of their existence. It was present in their lives, but as an intensity that was conditioned by either the collective informal solidarities of their colleagues and by individual strategies of resistance that they had developed to make and find meaning in their work. I return to that research later in this book to provide a case study of alienation and wellbeing. But that result was interesting, and it helped me answer one doubt I had about alienation as a totalizing vision of human existence, of presenting a zero-sum game where embodied human beings are dominated, lacking any subjectivity or agency, and alienation becomes a juggernaut sweeping away all that lies before it, where the subject is territorialized by this oppressive and omnipotent force.

Waite (2006), for example, in her research with agricultural workers in Maharashtra, India, makes the telling observation that while the workers may not have formal control over the production process and thereby could be seen as alienated, within a Marxian framework they still found some joy and value in the work they were doing. It is also a point made by Fanon (2021a) in *Black Skins, White Faces* that humans can retain agency in the face of extreme alienating conditions as created by colonialism and capitalism. That despite having just about everything humanizing stripped away, social agents can still resist and seek meaning in their everyday lives, attempting to create their own forms of identity and self, and are not simply overwhelmed by a totalizing alienating force.

Given that Marx devoted so much of his time and writings to how working-class people resist and, hopefully, attempt to overthrow capitalism, this position is untenable. Humans are highly capable of reflexivity and insight. That point is very clearly advanced in Marx's anthropology as discussed elsewhere in this book. Humans can interpret what is occurring around them and what is happening to them, and with that agency devise strategies and ways of being in the world that offer meaning. As musician Ian Curtis said in an interview with *NME* journalist Paul Rambali (1979) about his time prior to his success with Joy Division, 'I used to work in a factory, and I was really happy because I could daydream all day.' What the young Ian Curtis was alluding to, and what I found in my research with social workers, and Waite (2006) found in their research with agricultural workers, was what Lordon (2014) raises in his Spinozist commentary on alienation: affects matter. There can be moments of joy, of some form of realization that can provide compensation, albeit a fragile, fleeting one that can be taken away at an instant as Jackie in the introductory vignette had experienced.

The experience of alienation therefore needs to be understood with greater nuance. It is a state of being that emerges through multiple relations where the alienating tendencies of life in capitalism are conditioned by countervailing tendencies of varying relations, that while not being able to overcome the main tendency, alienation in this case, nevertheless, modulate, perhaps neutralize, how that tendency operates. Greaves' (2016) theory of 'cycles of alienation' is useful in developing this point. He rejects interpretations of alienation that cast it as 'fixed and frozen'. He advocates instead a more dynamic interpretation of alienation. As he says: 'The character of alienation is fluid, its moments determined by, among other things, the imperatives of capital, working class activity and social power, ideology and historical circumstances' (Greaves 2016: 51). This quotation needs to be broken down and its points teased out. Greaves draws attention to how the moments of alienation are determined by other relations. It is within the labour process that the cycles of alienation begin, according to Greaves. The labour process has always been a site of class conflict. Marx devotes a considerable part of *Capital I* to discussing workers' campaigns for a ten-hour day, and 'the nibbling and cribbling' of capital into workers' time to further maximize surplus value and to wrest further domination over work. Braverman's (1998) highly influential contribution to the sociology of work focuses on how management furthers its control over the labour process by implementing practices and procedures that routinize every activity of workers. All aspects of the labour process for Braverman (1998: 86) were thus 'devised, precalculated, tested, laid out, assigned and ordered and checked and inspected, and recorded throughout its duration and upon completion'. This development created a parallel paper trail of the actual physical labour process: the more management reconfigured the labour process in this way, the greater the loss of skill experienced by the worker.

Though the tendency over time has been in capital's favour, workers have won, in some countries, rights and control over their time in the form of the weekend, as an example. Resistance need not be the strike and the picket line as traditionally understood in the Marxist imaginary. Fleming and Sewell (2002) have also drawn attention to '*švejkism*'. Humour, an ironical disposition, and performing busyness while getting away with doing as little possible, are the modalities of this form of mundane everyday resistance.

The Golden Age of alienation literature can also add support to Greaves' proposition of cycles of alienation, and my observations on the contingency of alienation. That body of work reveals empirical research that identifies a far from uniform experience of alienation. Certain relations are mooted in the literature, which hold the potential to influence the experience, intensity and recognition of alienation. These contingencies include, for example, levels of social support in terms of relationships with colleagues or trade union membership (Pearlin 1962; Neal and Seeman 1964); wider social and national contexts (Seeman 1967); job size (Shepherd 1970); the extent of centralization within an organization (Aiken and Hage 1966); and bureaucratic and structural culture (Miller 1967). An appreciation of the role of consciousness and agency is also evident in dealing with and interpreting responses to being alienated or working in potentially alienating conditions (Barakat 1969; Blackburn and Mann 1979).

The work of Coburn (1979) is especially instructive in arguing for alienation as he centred on the relations between alienation and wellbeing in his research in a North American workplace of 2,180 workers. In line with much of the other empirical material of the time, he adopts a mass survey approach and the use of Likert scales to elicit data from the workers. Coburn rejects the eclectic approach of Seeman that is favoured by many of his empirical contemporaries and instead adopts an out-and-out Marxist framework that guides both the research design and interpretation of results. Coburn (1979: 42) interprets Marxism alienation theory as being a 'syndrome of characteristics', from which he selects monotonous work and control as being the two elements on which he decides to focus.

The results of the survey do indicate that some form of a relationship between alienation and wellbeing exists. However, the relationship is, as Coburn states, equivocal. The reasons for this less than strong result reflect the points made in this chapter concerning other empirical work that alienation is not a unitary experience. Once again, the relationship is not a simple binary phenomenon where someone *is*, or *is not*, alienated. There appear instead to be different intensities of alienation that are influenced by how much control a worker can exert over their work, how challenging and interesting that work is, and how congruent a fit there is between the abilities of an individual worker and the tasks they encounter in the workplace. Where there is greater nonalignment between ability and task, and where there is greater prevalence of monotonous tasks, the stronger the linkage between alienation and poor wellbeing. There is one further nuance, he adds, and that is psychological health and happiness, which are more likely to be affected than physical health.

Alienation is *almost* total for Fromm too. There are moments where social agents can find release or respite. He cites a number of small-scale activities that are not dissimilar to what Sennett (2008) has discussed on finding actualization in craft activities. However, not all activities that may seem to produce happiness, or joyful affects, provide that space beyond alienation. He is particularly scornful of consumer culture, a point of critique common to other writers associated with the Frankfurt School.

We must also include Zahar's (1974) critical discussion of Fanon. She expands, in a series of highly concise essays, on how a social agent is brought into the nexus of capitalist exploitation is critical in understanding how alienation is experienced. While Fanon is insightful in relation to the psychological effects of alienation and colonialization, given his background in psychiatry, and how it damages people, Fanon is on less sure footing, she notes, as to the economic aspects of alienation in colonialism and she advances a succinct discussion of how the economic aspects of colonialization can be added to Fanon to enrich his analysis.

The colonized subject possesses a different history to that of the worker in Europe. While both are subject to exploitation, how that occurred within the genesis of capitalism entails different consequences. As capitalism expanded across Europe in the 1700s, the old peasantry was subjected to a host of brutal disciplinary techniques where the slightest infringement of embryonic capitalist norms was met with execution or dehumanizing corporal punishments (Linebaugh 2003). The result of this terror was to produce a new capitalist subjectivity amenable to the demands of factory labour. For the colonized worker their entry into capitalist relations was through the occupation of their homeland and subsequent forced labour or enslavement into colonial and then capitalist production.

As such, Zahar (1974) argues, that specific history results in different relations to commodity production and therefore alienation. The exchange of commodities is a fundamental aspect of capitalist society. It is what provides a cohesion and structure for the capitalist system. For the colonized worker there is no commodity exchange within their society, it occurs on the world market with the flow of their labour heading towards the metropole. Zahar summarizes this relationship as follows:

> The alienation brought by colonialism is thus a double one. While in Capitalism the exploitation takes place in the realm of production and while the exchange keeps at least a semblance of equivalence, the colonized is exploited twofold: first in his conditions of production by the colonial overlord, and secondly in his exchange relations by the metropolis. (Zahar 1974: 13)

Without the integrative relations existing that are found in the Global North, how are colonialized workers kept within capitalism? The answer for Zahar (1974: 13) is that 'racial ideology assumes a special function and becomes an indispensable instrument in ensuring the cohesion of the colonial system, which is based on violence'. She was writing 40 years ago, and the commodity relations that she draws attention to as being a point of difference in colonized territories are increasingly evident in former colonized territories. But history still retains an influence and the material circumstances of different groups of workers are shaped by their relationship with the colonial past.

Alienation should therefore be seen as a *tendency* in capitalism, albeit a very strong one, emerging from the various relations that exist within workplaces and communities. Now obviously the concept of tendency is associated with Marx's economic writings in the *Theory of the Tendency of the Rate of Profit to Fall*. His analysis of capital was that it would, over the long term, be unable to sustain profitability. But he did not regard that decline as a linear process. Countervailing tendencies such as an increase in the exploitation of labour, foreign trade, cheapening of fixed capital, immiseration of workers, could stave off the decline, though only for so long. At the end of the day profit cannot be sustained, thereby leading to crisis for the capitalist system. The theory, as with every aspect of Marxism, is highly debated. I am not interested in that debate for the purposes here – but a good defence of *Tendency of the Rate of Profit to Fall* can be found in Carchedi and Roberts (2022). What I want to take is the central premise that within capitalism certain relations prevail in a dialectical relationship with each other from which emerges a regularity of some form.

Tendency can be a tricky concept to define in Marx as he used the term in different and inconsistent ways throughout his work and to refer to different events (Reuten 1997, 2004, 2014). Any recourse to Humean notions of causality, and to place the Marxist concept of tendency in that tradition, needs to be discounted. A tendency for Hume is a mere conjunction of events – this happened, and then this happened which, in turn, led to this outcome. A Humean law of causality for alienation would read something like: workers have no control over the labour process, no control over the object of production, they are therefore alienated because of the presence of the previous conditions. That depiction of alienation is banal and reductive and does not convey the complexity of alienation. It is also a mode of positivist or empiricist thinking which, as Fleetwood (2012) warns, does not belong to the Marxist dialectical tradition. Fleetwood (2012: 247) instead proposes one way of thinking about tendency that I follow here: '"tendency" is used to refer, metaphorically speaking, to something that powers, forces, drives, propels, pushes, presses, shoves, thrusts, exerts pressure, and so on'. This interpretation of tendency is trans-factual, which Fleetwood explains as:

> The tendency does not refer to the outcomes of something, like regular patterns in the flux of events. To put matters starkly, a tendency could be in operation even if no events were occurring and/or being (potentially) observed, because the tendency might be neutralised by (countervailing) tendencies coming from some other thing(s). (Fleetwood 2012: 247)

Let me rephrase this quotation to be about alienation. Alienation should not be seen as a regular pattern that exists like the signals emitting from a pulsar spaced at 1.33 seconds apart, but as a phenomenon possessing the potential to occur – evident in the poor wellbeing of workers in this case – but that can be affected by other relations and powers that can either neutralize it or alter the experience and intensity. What would those countervailing tendencies be?

The preceding discussion identified quite a few based on both Greaves and material from the Golden Age. They are listed here, but this should not be read as a definitive account, but indicative of what could exert some form of countervailing power at different scales within a workplace or community, or even wider society:

- *Ideology* – the difference, for example, between social democracy and neoliberalism. The shift from the former to the latter in many nations witnessed, as is well recorded elsewhere, an attack on workers' rights and the gains that workers and progressive movements had made since the 1960s. In the workplace neoliberalism heralded in new forms of technocratic management. They flexed their power through disciplinary metrics of measuring, monitoring and evaluating all aspects of the workplace, not just as some form of souped-up Fordism, but with the intention of forming new forms of individuated subjectivity more compliant with the needs of capital.
- *Workers' power* – levels of trade union membership and representation by political parties who can act in the collective interest of working people. In countries where trade union membership is higher and more organized then working conditions and the unequal relations between capital and worker can be modified in some way. In unionized industries workers' conditions and pay are better and higher than in those that are mot unionized.
- *Individual micro-acts of resistance* – the '*švejkism*' of Fleming and Sewell (2002), where individual workers try to make something out of their working day that retains for them some level of control or value that makes for a more tolerable time at work.
- *Joyful affects and moments of realization* – that within the labour process or within an individual's life more generally moments exist where the social agent can find some compensatory affect (a feeling of happiness or contentment, for example) that somehow makes up for the negative experiences they encounter.
- *Solidarity between workers and other social agents* – at the level of the workplace or community, where people support each other. Support can be affective or instrumental, simple acts like helping someone out who is overwhelmed or experiencing stress make a difference.
- *National context and culture* – nation states are the outcome of long histories of class and other conflicts, such as colonialism. That history creates different relationships between capital and labour. In some nation states, the Nordic countries for example, national culture has been described

as statist individualism (Berggren and Trägårdh 2011), where individual welfare is promoted collectively by the state. However, it needs to be said that this is far from socialism, but a variant of capitalism. Kanungo (1990) makes a similar point concerning wider context. He upbraids alienation theorists for a lack of awareness of the historical specificities of countries and nations.

- *Historical and colonial relations* – as argued by Fanon and Zahar, colonial and post-colonial relationships matter: how workers are historically incorporated into the exploitative nexus of capitalist relations influences their experiences.
- *Automation and technology* – in his classic work on alienation and automation, Blauner (1964) claimed that innovative automation and technology could reduce the alienation experienced by workers. Hardt and Negri return to this theme of technological liberation in their work on immaterial labour where knowledge workers possess skills and connectivity that will allow them to transcend capital. However, technology works in two directions. The considerable work of Thomson and colleagues analysing the experiences of call centre workers might suggest that the role of technology is more complex. In that body of research technology is far from liberating or de-alienating. It creates new forms of control, with a switch from dark Satanic mills to 'bright satanic offices' (Baldry et al 1998). As Greaves (2016: 54) also points out: 'The direction and codification of technological development comes from capital and is motivated by control.' Technology could be the worker's friend, as Bastani (2018) enthuses, but it exists within a pre-existing field of power relations.

One further point to make here: a vital temporal difference with the use of tendency as I am promoting for alienation exists in comparison with its use in *Tendency of the Rate of Profit to Fall*. The tendency of the rate of profit to fall occurs over long arcs of time, while tendency used here in relation to alienation occurs in the constant present.

Work takes many forms

Work is mentioned a great deal in this chapter and elsewhere. I want to make it clear that I am not only referring to work as in the paid relationship of employer and employee. Work takes many forms within capitalist society. A great deal of which is hidden from view, or, as Hatton (2015) frames it, 'invisibilized'. The work of women and racialized minority groups is often subject to invisibilization.

Hatton (2015) explores how a variety of social processes create boundaries around various forms of work. These boundaries render some forms of work visible and legitimate (typically paid market work) while invisibilizing others (typically the work of marginalized groups). She also provides a framework for understanding the process of invisibilization (Hatton 2017). It relies on the operation of three overlapping, but analytically separate, mechanisms.

The first mechanism is sociocultural. Invisibilization is enacted through the naturalizing and devaluing of the skills and activities of workers. By mobilizing, for example, gendered, racial and class ideologies, domestic and care work is constructed not as work but as an activity that women naturally and willingly perform.

The second mechanism is sociolegal. Certain forms of work are denied legitimacy and status by being situated outside the waged-work nexus. A sizeable amount of work is therefore deemed noneconomic and external to legal employment frameworks, which afford workers both rights and status. Various forms of work are invisibilized by this mechanism. For example, any voluntary work is not constructed as work on the basis that a social agent is offering their services for free or in the pursuit of personal goals. Domestic and care work is also invisibilized through this mechanism. It is not legally or technically categorized as work and its status is diminished as a result.

The third mechanism is socio-spatial. Where work is rendered invisible when conducted outside spaces that are constructed as workplaces. Work in the home is the classic example of spatial invisibilization. The home is not commonly understood as a place of work. In the Global North the home is traditionally constructed as a private sphere, apart and separate from work, a site of emotional and familial reproduction. Therefore, any activities that occur in the household cannot be work according to this exploitative sleight of hand.

Destabilizing definitions and accepted interpretations of work is not a new departure. Debates in the 1970s generated by Marxist and socialist feminist critiques of domestic labour allowed insights into how unpaid domestic labour is an integral relation in the social reproduction of labour essential for capitalist accumulation (Vogel 2013; Pettinger 2019). Feminists in the 1990s working within the feminist political economy paradigm drew further attention to how the work of women in various social spheres was ignored by mainstream economics. Waylen (1997), for example, has argued that mainstream economics is malestream economics, relying on a reductionist – if not idealist – rational actor anthropology. Social actors are constructed as set out to logically maximize their gains unhindered by any social or other constraints. Such a perspective occludes the work of women and many other marginalized and minority groups.

One form of invisible work that is being brought out more is 'illness-related work'. Pritlove et al (2019) describe it broadly as disease-management and avoidance of progression, as well as engaging with healthcare providers, all in addition to dealing with the everyday demands in managing family life and, in some cases, caring responsibilities or looking after or supporting others on an informal, unpaid basis due to long-term physical or mental problems, disability or old age. Despite being viewed as 'hard', 'overwhelming' and a 'full-time job' (Parsons et al 2008), such work is very often hidden and unsupported (Pritlove et al 2019). For me, the invisibilization that Hatton has brought to the fore is a form of alienation. It is the alienation from others, a complete non-recognition of the value and identity of people engaged in highly useful labour.

Conclusion

The experience of alienation for an embodied emotional human emerges out of the economic and social relations of capitalism. It arises because of a loss of control over the labour process and the object of production and the denial of reflective creativity. However, it is not a totalizing experience. Borrowing a term from Marxist economics, alienation is a *tendency* within capitalism which, when in effect, is powerful and a common experience. That tendency can be subject to neutralizing or modulating countervailing tendencies that reflect the power and strategies of individual and collective workers alongside other tendencies such as historical and national context.

The sketch of alienation that I have presented in this chapter has not answered criticisms of the theory have arisen over the years in relation to essentialism, species imperialism and, of course, Althusser's bold claim that alienation was a passing phase of Feuerbachian fancy for the young Marx.

Copyright notice

2

Responding to Criticisms
of Alienation Theory

Introduction

A great deal of time has elapsed since Marx first laid down his ideas on alienation in the *Economic and Philosophic Manuscripts* in 1844. A considerable volume of scholarship, theorization and empirical work on Marx and alienation has occurred since then, alongside various waves of theories and other work within the social sciences. Different theories and philosophies have raised interesting and challenging questions for how Marx understood alienation. Post-structuralism and post-modernism have posed questions as to what it is to be human. In those philosophies (and I am speaking very broadly here) any reference to some form of essence, a human nature, was eschewed for a fluid relative subjectivity that emerges from discourses and technologies of power. Essentialism is now a cardinal sin, to the point of it being 'a dirty word in the academy' according to Nussbaum (1992: 205). Anything that hints of some form of fixity or essence is automatically deigned to be faulty. The accusation of essentialism can be levelled against alienation theory, and, given the prominence I placed on human nature in Chapter 1, that charge requires a response. More recently, post-humanism and neo-materialism have queried the relationship between humans and nature, alongside the modernist impulse to privilege and centre humans (and a White, heterosexual, able-bodied, cis-male human at that) in understanding societies or environmental change. Those perspectives have sought to reorientate nature, from a passive inert entity that does nothing without human input to one that possess its own agential potentials. Those are good points and again require a response.

The challenges to alienation theory I just mentioned sit outside the Marxist tradition. Challenges also exist from *within* the Marxist literature as well. The intervention of Althusser and his project to rid Marxism of any of what he regarded as the damaging vestiges of Feuerbachian Humanism is the obvious one. He claimed, borrowing from Bachelard, that an 'epistemological break' exists in Marx. This break occurs in 1845 when the focus of Marx 's problematic shifts from a focus on the damage visited by capitalism on a human essence to a problematic concerned with the relations and means of production. The break has consequences for alienation theory. It lies on the wrong side of the break, the implication being that it is a concept that Marx himself abandoned. Even though the influence of Althusser has waned, the idea of the break, and the consequent dropping of alienation theory, remains pervasive and is seen by many, as Jaeggi observes, as axiomatic. That point too needs to be addressed.

Tackling the issues

For the remainder of this chapter, I wish to turn attention to answering the main criticisms of alienation theory, and in doing so expand and add to the theory of alienation. I begin by tackling the thorny issue of an essentialist human nature lurking in the background of alienation theory. This issue is vital to answer, as Byron (2013) makes clear: no theory of human nature (essence), no theory of alienation – there must be some *thing* that provides the friction for suffering to occur. I lay out that what various others have termed a thin or vague essentialism exists before proceeding to discuss more what a Marxist human nature could look like. Attention then turns to reflecting on humanity's relationship with nature and the problems that some Marxists and some readings of Marx create by offering an overly productivist and anti-ecological perspective. I then finish with one issue that has probably witnessed the most ink being spilt in Marxism: did the mature Marx dispense with alienation theory in his later work?

Human nature

Since the adoption of post-modernism within sociology anything that smacks of essentialism is automatically deemed to be regressive or reactionary. Essence connotes not acknowledging difference, of positing a false universalism and, at worst, opening the door to constructs of human nature that hold humans as selfish and mean. Indeed, human nature, or the idea of a human essence, is often associated with the political right. In Adam Smith humans are held to 'naturally truck, barter and exchange', inferring that people are natural capitalists, and therefore capitalist society is a natural state of affairs, and cannot be altered or transformed in any way. The right-wing interpretation of humanity reaches its apogee in the works of the science-fiction author Ayn Rand (1943, 1957) – a central influence in current American Libertarianism – with her objectivist philosophy, and in the dismal economics of Ludwig von Mises. As Duggan (2019) argues,

Rand inverted conventional notions of morality and in her work selfishness and greed are promoted as the most desirable of all virtues, nothing else demonstrates any value but the self-centred subject out to create his destiny (and it is usually *his* destiny) at the expense of anyone else. The moral worth of an individual is judged on how much dollar worth someone creates in their life. Any reference, for Rand, to altruism or working for the greater good of others is castigated as immoral collectivism. Her human nature is of the rapacious, self-centred, calculating individual out to maximize their wealth unconstrained by either the state or concern for others.

When appeals to human nature are mobilized, they often also lack any historical evidence to validate and support the model of human nature that is being advanced. Typically, as in the case of objectivism, a description of human nature is proposed that is either a description of the prevailing relations between people or an idealized human nature that aligns with the political perspective that the author endorses. Actual evidence of human nature is a little more complex. Recent work by Graeber and Wengrow (2021) articulates a range of anthropological and archaeological evidence in their assessment of what it is to be human. They are quite firm in their judgement on what life was like in the deeper history of humanity: 'There was no truly original state of affairs' (Graeber and Wengrow 2021: 140). What they find is that historical human societies are complex and very fluid. It is impossible to say that there was ever one way of doing society, one way of being human that represents a pure starting point of blissful utopia that for various reasons descends into the hierarchical hell of capitalist modernity, or one where humans have been capitalist entrepreneurs in waiting.

The work of Geras (1985) begins to answer the question of human nature from a Marxist perspective. He builds his case by logically interrogating Marx's *Sixth Thesis on Feuerbach* where he establishes that human nature becomes manifested in the various social relations that human society has developed over time before, second, identifying and marshalling textual support from subsequent writings of Marx. Geras establishes that Marx did advance a theory of human nature that outlines a distinct philosophical anthropology of humanity, and that there are certain transhistorical aspects of humanity that are an indelible and fundamental part of being human that in turn are expressed in different historical forms over time. Those attributes and capacities essentially form a dynamic inter-relationship of capacities and needs, which allow humans as part of the natural world not just simply to exist but to progress through time creating and innovating new and higher ways of existing.

Geras (1985) makes a strong case that this Marxian theory of human nature occupies more than a secondary, or peripheral role, within the whole framework of Marx's theories. For Geras it is fundamental to the whole project of historical materialism, providing both the why and the how of historical and social change:

> [H]istorical materialism itself, this whole distinctive approach to society that originates with Marx, rests squarely upon the idea of a human nature. It highlights that specific nexus of universal needs and capacities which explains the human production process and man's organised transformation of the material environment; which process and transformation it treats in turn as the basis both of the social order and of historical change. (Geras 1985: 108)

So, what is involved in this specific nexus of relations of universal needs and capacities alluded to in this quotation from Geras? These are developed in greater depth in this section, but essentially, they consist of:

- Humans are embodied beings who are part of, and live in relation to, nature, and have distinct biological needs that are expressed in different historical forms over time. Geras (1985: 83) provides a general schedule of them which reads as follows: 'food, clothing, shelter, fuel, rest and sleep; hygiene, "healthy maintenance of the body", fresh air and sunlight; intellectual requirements, social intercourse, sexual needs ... support specific to the needs of infancy, old age, and incapacity, and the need for a safe and healthy working environment.'
- Humans have an innate capacity or potentiality to creatively labour on the natural world in which they exist in order to meet those biological and historical needs.
- Humans also labour cooperatively in relation to other humans. Without that ability to be social, then humans would be isolated beings.
- Humans also have the capacity to consciously reflect, symbolically interpret and enact change on the world around them.

I expand on the points concerning labour, the capacity to consciously reflect, and work cooperatively in separate sections shortly, but for now I tackle the general question of essences and essentialism.

Foucault (1997: 282) has strongly criticized alienation and any claims that 'there exists a human nature or a base that, as a consequence of certain historical, economic, and social processes, has been concealed, alienated, or imprisoned in and by mechanisms of repression'. For him, alienation is a state that cannot exist as it denotes a self beyond the disciplines of power. Subjectivity can only come into being in his philosophy by it being constituted by power, with no prior subject existing that can one day be liberated and set free. This position is an unsatisfying aspect of Foucault which arises out of his avid anti-humanism: the subject is written out of his work, replaced by humans who are simply the effects of discourses, constituted by power and deprived of any agential capacities. As Brenner (1994) points out, the eradication of the subject is a logical outcome of the specific functionalist framework that Foucault constructs: the social is the self-assembling of power that appears to float free of the actions of any specific human subject. By negating the subject in this way, Foucault sets up a further problem for himself. One of his other major claims is that power is always accompanied by resistance, that the two are an indissoluble dyad, and that power can never enjoy free reign as it always spontaneously creates resistance, and that resistance is the practice of free subjects. The sheer weight of his writing on power leaves resistance as a poor second, existing as a theoretical sketch and lacking the deep layers of empirical work that accompanies descriptions of power. Foucault's specific form of functionalism therefore removes the subject as anything but a passive constituent of power and at best we find a contradictory position on who it is that actually does the resisting.

The later Foucault (1990, 1998a, 1998b), as evident in the *History of Sexuality*, does attempt to bring back the subject, but his rendering of the subject is essentially a weak revisiting of Nietzsche's understanding of the subject and the boundless creative processual self that he lays down (Callinicos 1999). What Foucault and Nietzsche both miss is that the subject cannot exist in such an unlimited state and that history conditions (both positively and negatively) where someone can take their life. They are also short on what is it about humans, what capacities they possess, that allow them to act on both themselves and the world in which they live. For example, Foucault urges that social beings can become art, but to be an artist (or more specifically an artist of the self) one must first possess the capacities to think creatively or to be able to reflect upon the act itself, and the ability to act and alter the self: none of which is present in Foucault in any degree nor can be constructed from his writings in a similar way that Geras has performed for Marx.

It is just not those, such as Foucault and other post-structuralists, from outside the Marxist tradition that level the accusation of essentialism against alienation theory. Plenty of Marxists prosecute alienation theory on grounds of essentialism too. Althusser (1969) is the best known, and I return to him and his 'epistemological break' later. The once dominant school in the 1980s of Analytical Marxism, associated with Elster (1985) and Cohen (2001) embarked on a similar mission. Cohen had a particular disdain for anything that smacked of Hegel, or essence, going as far to state in very unscholarly terms that Hegelian concepts such as Spirit (*Geist*), and any other reading of Marxism that did not correspond to his interpretation of Marxism, were 'bullshit'. In fact, Geras (1985), a proponent of human nature in Marx, noted a long list of Marxists who have disavowed a role for human nature or some form of essence within Marx: 'Tom Bottomore, Robert D. Cumming, Eugene Kamenka, Louis Althusser, Vernon Venable, Robert Tucker, Kate Soper, Colin Summer, and Sidney Hook; to name but a few.'

I respond to this charge of essentialism by claiming an essentialism of sorts exists in Marx, and all the better for it, as ultimately it makes for a more coherent theory of alienation. Let us begin with Meikle (1985) and his take-no-prisoners defence of essentialism in Marx before incorporating more recent developments. Meikle offers a distinctive perspective on Marx's essentialism. Rather than trying to shy away from any charge of essentialism and trying to dilute or modify what Marx says about essentialism, Meikle instead embraces essentialism and makes the strong claim that an essentialism is present within Marx. Meikle draws on the Aristotelian influences on Marx in his defence of Marx's essentialism. Aristotle is an under-appreciated influence on Marx. Hegel is often regarded as the main – if not only – guiding star in Marx's philosophy. But as a number of commentators note, Aristotle's philosophy shaped Marx too (see Blackledge 2012; Levine 2021) and it is an influence returned to in greater depth in Chapter 3 when attention turns to alienation and wellbeing.

For Meikle (1985), the essentialism evident in Marx is one vibrant with movement, that acknowledges fluidity, and where transformations can and do occur. What he argues, in some respects, does not chime with what is commonly understood as essentialism: that essence is an internal, if not mystical, transhistorical fixed and frozen entity incapable of change. The defensive play of Meikle is quite simple: things have a shape. That's what he really means by an essence. All things possess a series of relationships that make them what they are. Accepting the existence of an essence does not obviate or exclude any idea of change. It does not say that things are fixed forever and ever, but rather within whatever is under consideration a set of relationships exist that make it what it is. McLennan (1996) also makes a similar point. If things did not have some essential properties, they would not be recognizable. He advocates a rehabilitation of essentialism that is weaker than Meikle's strong essentialism, but:

> note that this is only a qualification of essentialism, not a refutation, because if we are in any way committed to 'structural' styles of explanation, then we are compelled at some point to decide, in principle at any rate, *which tendencies in a complex process lie at the heart of that process and which do not.* Any theory which has interesting and bold things to say about social structure and social change must be essentialist; it will identify central concepts to 'pick out' purported key mechanisms and forces within a complex whole. (McLennan 1996: 66, emphasis added)

I like that he draws attention to what he terms tendencies that lie at the heart of a process. We need to identify what makes something possible, what are the relations, the creative relations, that make something what it is. There can be other relations/tendencies involved at a particular point in time, but these are not so important when considering what are the fundamental relationships. Part of McLennan's argument draws on Nussbaum (1993), who, like Meikle (1985), constructs a defence of essentialism guided by Aristotle. Nussbaum has developed a considerable body of work since then, advocating her capabilities approach. In that early work she identifies two levels of her vague thick theory of human essence. The first level turns on physical functioning of the body with its need for shelter, food and comfort. The second level concerns maximizing the capacities that humans possess to lead a full, productive and actualized life.

Fanon (2021a) had no hesitation in placing a human essence at the heart of his writings on alienation. Colonialism and capitalism had stripped away what it was to be Black and replaced the 'black essence' with a series of White performativities. As part of any anti-colonial and anti-capitalist struggle Fanon calls for a critical return to pre-colonial African history and culture (Rabaka 2009). This position may smack of a very strong essentialism: some form of pure Africanism consisting of fixed exclusive traits, just waiting to be (re)discovered once the yoke of colonialism is lifted. As Nielsen (2013) argues, however, this is far from the case. The essence that Fanon mobilizes works like Spivak's (1988) strategic essentialism, that Nielsen (2013: 349) defines as 'the oppressed group, recognizing its need for group unity and a positive self-conception, intentionally promotes an essentialist identity'.

On one level, Fanon's essentialism therefore operates as a political tactic in the struggle against colonialism and alienation. The erasure of colonial interiority is an essential element of overcoming colonialism and alienation and calling for another way of being that replacing colonialism's the erasure of identity and self. Strategic essentialism as Nielsen points out is not a reactionary romanticism but one that can allude to other forms of being in the past that can inform the future, not by returning or replicating the past but providing ideas on how existence can be different.

That form of essentialism is a useful tactic that can be made universal to some extent. As Fisher claims with his concept of capitalist realism, one aspect of life under contemporary capitalism is the totalizing presence of capitalist relations, to the point where there seems no alternative exists. A strategic essentialism can point to other ways of being that stand outside the narratives and ideologies of capitalism.

More recent proponents of alienation theory have similarly adopted a weak or vague essentialism. Øversveen (2022 452) in his defence of alienation endorses a ' "thin" conception of essence that emphasizes our capacity for development, change and reinvention'. A definite theme is evident in the authors surveyed in this discussion of human nature, essence and essentialism: an essence exists but it is one that is qualified with an adjective such as weak, vague or thin. Perhaps this phrasing is too defensive, as what is referred to are highly important aspects of being human or capacities that are quite powerful in how they place humans in relation to nature and history. But, nevertheless, it is useful to conceptualize essence in this way as it avoids making reference to some anterior, pure or authentic self that humans must return to in order to begin living a life free of alienation.

The following provides a metaphor of the type of human essence I am suggesting. Taking a cue from McLennan, I compare human essence to football: what is the essence of football?[1] There must be players, a ball, a pitch and some agreement on what the rules are, specifically that the ball is kicked rather than handled. These elements in the parlance of internal relations constitute the relations of football. It is the relations that provide the overall shape of the game. In the weaker or vague, following Nussbaum, form of essentialism proposed here the essence of football does not mean that every pitch must be the San Siro stadium, with its immaculate striped pitch, banks of seating and so on. Anyone who has ever kicked a ball about as a child will have used jumpers for goalposts in the local park. The youngsters may have only set up one goal with no clear idea where the boundaries are to decide a throw-in. But anyone either sitting in the *Curva Sud* or walking through a municipal park would instantly recognize that a game of football is underway. One could even time travel to the late Victorian period when the game was first developing. What the time-traveller would have seen at that point in the game's development may look more akin to rugby, given it was much more physical at that stage, but the round ball, the teams and the goals would instantly tell you that a football match was underway. This form of essentialism also allows for flexibility and change. Remaining with the analogy, football is a constantly changing sport, how the game is played and the tactics used. The penalty box, a major feature of the modern game, and the deciding element within so many cup finals, only made an appearance in 1902.

What constitutes football can change over time and is constantly doing so. There is no final limit on what it can be, nor is there an end goal or telos. For example, three-sided football, as proposed by situationalist Asger Jorn, requires a hexagonal pitch with three teams playing more cooperatively than in the two-team game. Quite different from the current game but still recognizable as football.

This discussion has advocated what others have termed a thin or vague human essence agreeing in a distinct range of capacities, potentials or abilities.

---

[1]   I mean Association Football, what is sometimes referred to (irritatingly) as soccer.

But what are those abilities? Usually agreement exists as to labour, needs and the ability to consciously reflect and cooperate, but with little extension thereafter. The following sections add weight and specificity to that thin or vague essentialism.

Humans as embodied beings

Positing human beings as embodied is an important inclusion within alienation theory and any understanding of human nature or human essence. Most other commentators who make very cogent observations and analysis of alienation theory tend to elide a fundamental point that humans are embodied beings, who are fleshy, leaky, emotional, pained, fragile and vulnerable entities. Given that I will be talking later about wellbeing this point is vital to make as the materiality of the body is an essential relation within wellbeing.

The embodied and emotional turns within sociology at the turn of this century brought to the fore that too much of sociology had wandered into a Cartesian dualism (for summaries of this work, see Williams 1998; Bendelow and Willaims 2002). The social agents to whom sociologists referred seem to only exist as far as what they are thinking. When bodies were mentioned, they appeared as the outcomes of discourses and texts rather than as fleshy, natural, feeling, active and sensuous entities.

Drawing on a range of phenomenological literature such as Merle-Ponty (2002), the body began to (re)emerge within medical sociology. The body that eventually became visible was one that was simultaneously biological and social, that extended into social and material space. It was instantaneously *Körper* and *Leib*. *Körper* refers to the physical material and biological body, while *Leib* refers to the lived experience of the body in meeting others and existing within a social, cultural and historical context. Now this may seem like introducing a Cartesian dualism counterpointing the physical and the lived experience, but as Slatman (2014) argues, we can think of the body as *LiebKörper* – after all humans cannot have an existence and engage in a myriad of social relations without being a biological body. Even in what may seem the immateriality of cyberspace at some point there is a biological body sitting with a headset or in front of a computer.

Following on from the point about cyberspace, embodied humans have always existed in relation to other entities and in turn been shaped by them. Engels' famous meditation in *The Part Played by Labour in the Transition from Ape to Man* traces how the act of labour, of using flint and then ever more complex tools, shaped and formed the hand, allowing it to become something else, leading to 'the high degree of perfection required to conjure into being the pictures of a Raphael, the statues of a Thorwaldsen, the music of a Paganin'. But that change in the hand ripples through both the biological and social body of humans and nature, creating new technology, new ways of social interaction and being social. Engels here is drawing on his dialectical approach to causality, where one causality is not linear but loops around in a wider ensemble of internal relations:

> Further, we find upon closer investigation that the two poles of an antithesis, positive and negative, e.g., are as inseparable as they are opposed, and that despite all their opposition, they mutually interpenetrate. And we find, in like manner, that cause and effect are conceptions which only hold good in their application to individual cases; but as soon as we consider the individual cases in their general connection with the universe as a whole, they run into each other, and they become confounded when we contemplate that universal action and reaction in which causes and effects are eternally changing places, so that what is effect here and now will be cause there and then, and vice versa. (Engels 2015: 21)

The embodied human being is therefore not a completed project, one that is altering and alterable, becoming part of an ensemble of internal relations of bodies, minds, economic relations, things, nature and technologies. But what does Marx explicitly say about the embodied human activity?

In moving away from Hegel's overt idealism, Marx places himself very firmly as a materialist. Philosophically such a move carries many different implications. While for Hegel, bodies were important and definitely exist within his overall schema, in that their activities were the material manifestation of the Spirit's (*Geist*) journey through space and time in its great quest for realization through history, for Marx the human body as a sensuous emotional and biological body occupies a central place in his overall philosophical anthropology. Humanity is here anchored in the natural world, with humans exhibiting capacities, features and tendencies that can be found in non-human animals. As Fracchia (2005) notes, Marx grounds his materialism and his approach to human nature in a 'human corporeal organisation', where core elements of Marx's theories rely upon an inclusion of the capacities of the human body to undertake labour and of course to make history.

Extensive textual evidence exists within Marx to substantiate this point. I shall identify and highlight certain examples before focusing on their relevance to Marx's philosophy generally and to alienation in particular. Marxian materialism stands in contrast with Hegelian idealism, a move clearly visible within the *Manuscripts*, where Marx devotes several sections to distancing himself from Hegel by drawing on Feuerbach's criticism of Hegel. In the *Economic and Philosophical Manuscripts* numerous examples exist of Marx staking out of a materialist position. One of the clearest declarations of this intent appears in the Third Manuscript:

> Man is directly a natural being. As a natural being and as a natural living being he is on the one hand endowed with natural powers, vital powers – he is an active natural being. These forces exist in him as tendencies and abilities – as instincts. On the other hand, as a natural, corporeal, sensuous objective being he is a suffering, conditioned and limited creature, like animals and plants. (Marx 1977: 136)

It is just not in the earlier work of the young Marx that examples of an embodied sensuous human being appear. Throughout *Capital*, Marx maintains this anthropology of human activity. What is striking about it is that this notion of an embodied human social agent exercising their combined mental and physical self is not just a minor component or bit-player, but instead occupies an important position in a variety of theoretical pursuits. Consider the following passage from the chapter on labour power – a passage that Rees (1998) approvingly notes would sit quite comfortably in the *Manuscripts*:

> Labour is, first of all, a process between man and nature, a process by which man, through his own actions, mediates, regulates and controls the metabolism between himself and nature. He confronts the materials of nature as a force of nature. He sets in motion the natural forces which belong to his body, his arms, his legs, head and hands, in order to appropriate the materials of nature in a form adapted to his own needs. Through this movement he acts upon external nature and changes it, and in this way he simultaneously changes his own nature. (Marx 1990: 283)

In *Capital* chapter 10, on the working day, the philosophical position of the embodied human being appears once more, this time in connection with what Marx terms as the 'vital force', the natural physical limits of the human being and their intellectual requirements in a given day:

> Within the 24 hours of the natural day a man can only expend a certain quantity of his vital force. ... During the part of the day the vital force must rest, sleep; during another part the man has to satisfy other physical needs, to feed, wash and clothe himself. ... The worker needs time in which to satisfy his intellectual and social requirements, and the extent and the number of these requirements is conditioned by the general level of civilisation. (Marx 1990: 341)

These references to the embodied human agent are elements within some of Marx's economic analysis of how commodities acquire a certain value and their place within that analysis is critical. Unlike neoclassical economics with its focus on marginal utility, which states that it is supply and demand, and the subjective assessment of a commodity that sets the value of a commodity, Marx places the value of a commodity into a temporal context. Before anything else occurs, any commodity has to be produced before it enters the marketplace – hence labour theory of value, to describe his approach to the creation of value (Harman 2009).

Neoclassical economics does not comprehend this fact and suffers from the illusion that commodities somehow spontaneously appear in the marketplace without anyone having to actually initially produce the commodity. The value of the commodity for Marx is determined by the socially necessary cost of the labour that is involved in the production of the commodity. Part of that involves the amount paid to a worker, as a living being, who needs to be able to maintain their existence on a level that is both biologically and socially viable in order to be able to exert their labour power:

> However, labour-power becomes a reality only being expressed; it is activated only through labour. But in the course of this activity, i.e. labour, a definite quantity of human muscle, nerve, brain, etc. is expended, and these things have to be replaced. Since more is expended, more must be received. If the owner of labour-power works today, tomorrow he must again be able to repeat the same process in the same conditions as regards health and strength. (Marx 1990: 275)

At the heart of the economic engine, therefore, is a real-life human being. What we encounter in this mature work on economics is an analysis of value, but one built on the philosophy outlined in Marx's early years in the *Manuscripts* concerning the productive capacities of a natural therefore exhaustible being.

So, within Marx is the acceptance of an embodied biological human being. By having this understanding of humans, it therefore logically requires us to accept certain fundamental conditions of what it is to be human, replete with all the various physiological systems, strengths and weaknesses that entails. Marx makes note, for example, that being sensuous means to suffer, therefore we must accept that human beings possess not only the emotions of suffering but also the physiological systems that respond to pain and threat, such as the sympathetic nervous system. The presence of a fleshy, sensuous and emotional body is returned to in Chapter 3 as it plays a key role in alienation and wellbeing.

Needs

Following on from the previous point we also have to accept that humans as with any other non-human species possess a range of needs and are capable of exercising a range of capacities and potentials. However, what makes the human palette of needs and capacities different from other species is that they exhibit a much higher degree of dynamism and development than other non-human animal species. The majority of non-human animals remain in a historical stasis. What they need and how they can realize and meets those needs never really changes, and if it does, the change is by minute degrees over extended periods of time as opposed to the polar shifts over quite short periods of time in what humans deign as needs and the capacities they can exercise in order to meet those needs.

As Creaven (2000: 75–76) highlights, needs and capacities play a very distinct role within Marx's overall philosophy. Their interplay acts as a historical driver for human change and development by creating a continual spiralling looping exercise. The meeting of one need leads to the exercise of a capability and once that need is met, the material basis and social space is created for new needs to develop, which in turn require the enhancement of existing capacities in order to meet them:

> Now, the 'capacities' and 'tendencies' component is theoretically significant for Marx because it furnishes historical materialism with an explanation of how human society and socio-cultural is possible. The theoretical function of the 'needs' and 'interests' component of human nature, by contrast, is to furnish historical materialism with part of the explanation of why society and history have a dynamic. (Creaven 2000: 75–76)

What I wish to develop next is a narrative that human needs may historically begin as very closely tied to biological and natural functions of a limited order (food, shelter and so on as Marx notes in *The German Ideology*) but change and become increasingly historical and relative to the general development of a given society. This is a position marked out by Sayers (1998) who cautions against a neat binary divide between transhistorical needs and historically specific needs. He instead opts for a historicist approach that stresses that what begin as natural needs, and therefore transhistorical, are very rapidly transformed in the historical development of humanity; that way, the 'natural' baseline of a need is so reorganized that it loses any transhistorical reference point and is instead pegged to movements of history:

> By contrast, for Marx, I am suggesting, not only desires but also needs grow historically. What are luxuries for one generation become

necessities for the next. Some, at least, of these new needs are 'true' needs relative to the social conditions in which they arise, in that their satisfaction is necessary for a minimum standard of social life and happiness. (Sayers 1998: 134)

Some of those biological needs in turn become infused with the symbolic social needs. Eating provides a good example. There is a biological requirement to eat, but when humans eat, they do not simply refer to the nearest source of proteins, carbohydrates and vitamins, to meet the impulse of hunger. Instead, they turn to substances that have been socially and historically identified and designated as food. So, it is perfectly possible to meet one's protein needs by tickling a trout in a river stream, flipping it in the air, catching it and killing it, before biting into the flesh – except such a direct form of obtaining protein would not sit well with the modern Western mind, for instance. The fish would have to be prepared and cooked first, before it is symbolically interpreted as being food as opposed to being a rather unappetizing dead fish.

As Lebowitz (2003) argues, there is no real end to the needs that humans can create for themselves. Somewhere in the distance a 'bliss point ' (Lebowitz 2003: 43), as he refers to the moment of ultimate satiation of need, appears to exist, but it is utterly unobtainable since human creativity constantly brings forth both new social and socio-natural needs. Again, this need-creation and attempted need-satiation nexus provides a dynamic that drives change in both individual embodied humans and in the societies in which they live.

Human labour

Labour is a fundamental of Marx's philosophical anthropology. It is the defining aspect of being human, the species-being, what makes humans truly human. It is also through labour that the needs outlined in the previous section are met. Marx (1990: 133) describes the importance of labour in *Capital* as 'being a condition of human existence which is independent of all forms of society; it is an eternal natural necessity which mediates the metabolism between man and nature, and therefore human life itself'. Labour is therefore something that arches over time and existence, a true human universal transcendental capacity that is not locked into a specific time and place, but is ever present in human society.

Sayers (2007) provides a useful oversight of what Marx understood by labour. As with many of Marx's ideas the influence of Hegel is ever present, and it is useful to first inspect the relationship, similarities and differences between Hegel and Marx. Both of them perceived labour as being how humans are in the world and that it is labour that vitally progresses humans through history and, in turn, creates new ways of being human in addition to new forms of society. So, as Sayers (2007) notes, both Marx and Hegel are very similar in this respect. Some substantial differences do exist, however, in their understanding of labour, but these differences are made complex by the fact that Marx did not have full access to Hegel's writings on labour. Hegel's Jena lectures, where he outlines a radical critique of the emerging industrial form of capitalism, were not published until the 1930s. Had they been available to Marx, as Averini (1996) speculates, he may have made a different evaluation of Hegel's assessment of labour, given the similarity the young Hegel has with the young Marx. What Marx could draw on were the later works such as the *Phenomenology*, where Hegel's conservativism was beginning to be more pronounced. Marx is perhaps correct in describing Hegel's perspective on labour as being 'one-sided', as he does in the *Manuscripts*, and celebrating the universal nature of labour as self-realization without placing that labour in its historical context, therefore gaining a fuller 'double-sided' understanding of labour. There is one more fundamental difference between Marx and Hegel and that is found in regard to their different respective interpretations of the important moment of objectification (*Vergrgenständlichung*) that occurs during the labour process. For the idealist Hegel, such a moment was in itself alienation, as something that was part of the higher realm of ideas was placed into the lower realm of material entity, hence being a loss or separation; while for the materialist Marx, the creation of an object was an achievement, the moment when the human capacity to create was made visible and real within the ontological flow of history. Alienation is not the actual act of creation but what happens to the object of creation within its social and historical context – a point to be returned to later in this chapter. The noun 'object' by itself may strike a utilitarian or instrumental note, but for Marx the objects of human production are imbued with the consciousness of the maker and stand for much more than a simple thing or presence. Lefebvre captures how the object in Marxian thought exceeds mundane definitions:

> For child and adult alike, objects are not merely a momentary material presence, or the occasion of a subjective activity; they provide us with an objective social content. Traditions (technical, social spiritual) and the most complex qualities are present in the humblest of objects, conferring on them a symbolic value or 'style'. Each object is a content of consciousness, a moment. (Lefebvre 1968: 128)

Clarifying what an object means leads to another important aspect of defining what Marx meant by labour. Constant reference to objects and objectification, as Sayers (2007) notes, could be interpreted to mean that Marx had a very distinct 'productivist' model of work in mind when he deploys the term labour, implying steel bashing, factory production line and concrete physical objects. The charge against Marx has been led by Hardt and Negri (2005) and their assertion that a post-industrial world is now in operation that relies on what they term 'immaterial labour'. This new form of labour refers to computerized production, software programming and similar new technologies that do not produce material entities but immaterial entities such as knowledge and information. This perspective, according to Sayers (2007), does not withstand scrutiny. For Marx, labour was not so much about 'making' objects but rather about 'forming' them. Marx's emphasis on forming is yet another example of his Hegelian heritage, where the stress is on the dynamic progression of human labour and it achievements as opposed to isolating human labour at a particular temporal juncture.

Thus, the object of labour does not necessarily have to be a physical concrete object. It can be anything as long as it involves forming something, with that something being anything that effects a material change in the world and in the subjectivities of all involved. Sayers puts it thus:

> It is wrong to believe that 'symbolic' work creates only symbols or ideas – effects that are purely subjective and intangible. All labour operates by intentionally forming matter in some way. Symbolic labour is no exception: it involves making marks on paper, agitating the air and making sounds, creating electronic impulses in a computer system, or whatever. Only in this way is it objectified and realized as labour. In the process, it affects – creates, alters – subjectivity. All labour, it should be noted, does this. (Sayers 2007: 445)

The same can be said for emotional labour. There, too, no concrete entity is formed. However, some form of labour is objectified in the form of the marks on paper and making sounds as already mentioned, but emotions too are drawn from within and then objectified in the external world. This line of reasoning is also apparent in Hochschild's (1983) thesis of emotional labour, where she argues that emotional work is not so different from conventional physical labour in that the physical body (or labour power in Marxist coinage) is drawn upon to perform the job and to create an object, while in emotional labour the physical body is still drawn upon (but this time the emotional part of the body) to produce the required object, a satisfied customer.

The central point of this discussion is that for Marx, labour is about objectification but the emphasis should be on forming rather than producing what is objectified, with that object being anything from a concrete physical entity, to a series of symbols, or emotional displays.

Cooperative and social

Humans are by necessity social (*zoon politikon*) in that they exist with others and that cooperation is vital for human survival. That appeal to the cooperative though does not mean that humans are purely some variants of the Borg collective, where all desires and identity are subsumed into one undifferentiated mass. Marx advances a dialectical approach to understanding the relationships between the individual and the collective. We are formed through our interactions with others, shaping and being shaped by our intersubjectivity, which is simultaneously shaped by the historical and emplaced circumstances of existence.

Humans would be lost without other humans to be with, not simply in having no one with whom to talk, but also on a much deeper existential level. Without others, human selfhood and subjectivity could not exist. Human subjectivity, as Reed (2016) writes, is thoroughly transindividual, it is formed through the current and historic resolutions that people have with each other in their immediate circle and across the globe. We draw who we are not from internal desires and passions about who we want to be but instead from a common stock of symbols and cultures that are culturally and historically for us to select, reject or react against. The most obvious forms of such symbols are language. It is language that structures thought, providing the grammar for making assessments and claims about who we are.

Marx points in a different direction from Rousseau (1762), who in his philosophy of alienation held humanity in its primitive stage isolated as lone individuals, surviving by their individual activities in the natural forest. Marx also differs from the classical economists who he famously chides for presenting a Robinson Crusoe interpretation of individual humans as being marooned on their own little economic island. Humanity is fundamentally social. Indeed, in reviewing the brain from an evolutionary context, neuroscientists Cacioppo and Patrick (2008) have identified that elements of the modern human brain have evolved to make humans 'naturally' sociable: the neurochemical oxytocin playing a particular role in maintaining social cohesion by creating positive and pleasant sensations when humans are in the company of others.

Being social offers many advantages for the human species on a number of levels. The main advantage of sociability is that it allows mutual aid to develop, whereby one's own individual chances of survival are greatly increased by being able to draw upon the assistance of others.

Human consciousness

The discussion so far has emphasized that for Marx humans were to be found in nature and not in the world of ideas. In rejecting Hegel's idealism Marx progressed a material philosophy that accepted that humans exist as part of nature and are natural beings, conditioned by the various processes that entail and require a relationship with nature in order to survive. As Marx and Engels (1974: 48) famously noted in *The German Ideology*, 'But life involves before everything else eating and drinking, a habitation, clothing and many other things The first historical act is thus the production of the means to satisfy these needs, the production of material life itself'. Explicit here is a commitment to a realist position that an objective world (nature) exists external to the constructions of humanity and which also, in turn, exerts certain unavoidable requirements on humans in order for them to exist. What Marx also develops in his material philosophy, and in particular, in his anthropological philosophy, is an understanding of humans as *Homo faber*, as being in essence a being that can socially and reflectively labour.

This emphasis on humans being so intimately part of nature does pose one particular problem. An ontological danger could exist if accepting the existence of human consciousness leads to positing human beings as not being part of nature, but instead against (or beyond) nature – a slippage back into the idealism and over-subjectivity that Marx reprimanded Hegel for advancing. Taking such a position could lead to, or at least open the possibility of, a reductionist position on humans; that humans are bound genetically into nature, and as such humans would share the same impulsivities as animals; all of which would entail a fixed nature understanding of humanity. Humans, however, possess one critical capacity that differentiates them from nature: they possess consciousness. It is this capacity to reflect, plan and consider actions that differentiates humans from other species. In *Capital I* Marx makes his position on this clear in the following celebrated passage concerning the difference between human and animal activity (architects and bees, in this instance) within nature:

> We pre-suppose labour in a form that stamps it as exclusively human. A spider conducts operations that resemble those of a weaver, and a bee puts to shame many an architect in the construction of her cells. But what distinguishes the worst architect from the best of bees is this, that the architect raises his structure in imagination before he erects it in reality. At the end of every labour-process, we get a result that already existed in the imagination of the labourer at its commencement. He not only effects a change of form in the material on which he works, but he also realises a purpose of his own that gives the law to his modus operandi, and to which he must subordinate his will. (Marx 1990: 283–284)

Reflecting on this passage, what is important to note is that human activity for Marx is not just instinctual behaviour, where all activity is set, largely repetitive and follows a genetic 'blueprint'. Rather, human activity emerges out of the thought processes of a human purposefully reflecting on what they need to do in order to achieve a particular goal. That reflection is also crucially not just a singular event but exists within the flow of human history and human social interaction. So, when a human confronts nature in order to do something they are guided and informed by the previous human activity (the ideas of dead generations transmitted by culture), and current experiences of other humans beings. Human labour is therefore also cumulative. The temporally prior labour of other human beings in the main assists and improves the labour of other contemporary human beings. That is why, referring to this example, architecture and the design of the dwellings in which human beings live changes over time. The change from cave dwelling to wattle-and-daub to skyscrapers provides an illustration of how human labour brings about innovation, change and creativity in the objects that they create with nature. As wonderful and amazing as a beehive is, it still essentially takes the same form now that beehives have taken for the duration of the current species of bees: change and innovation for humans but relative fixity for other species.

There may be a suggestion in this quotation that Marx is slipping into some form of idealism. After all, it is the mind here that is projecting on the world and in turn shaping it. There are many ways to answer this question. Thoughts are material to some extent. They exist as electrical impulses in the matter of the brain and therefore are part of the material ensemble of a given situation in which a human exists. But, as Marx and Engels elaborate over a number of works, their materialism is not a simple mechanical materialism (Rees 1998). They see consciousness and material reality being mediated by human activity – labour more precisely – and that labour is the unity of materiality and consciousness.

To that end, Rees (1998: 73) quotes the following extract from Jakubowski (1990: 60):

> Consciousness no longer stands outside being and is no longer separated from its object. … Consciousness is determined by the transformations of being; but, as the consciousness of acting men, it in turn transforms, this being. Consciousness is no longer consciousness *above* an object, the duplicated 'reflection' of an individual object, but a constituent part of changing relations, which are what they are only in conjunction with the consciousness that corresponds to their material existence. Consciousness is the self-knowledge of reality, an expression and a part of the historical process of being, which knows itself at every stage of development.

That labour, that activity, occurs within a historical context. 'Ideas do not fall from heaven', as Labriola (2005: 155) stated. They exist within a context that is shaped by material reality and given by the history of previous mediated labour.

Relationship with nature

An assumption exists that Marx is antagonistic towards nature, an anti-ecological productivist that places humans above nature and casts nature as a passive resource that only exists for humans: possessing no life, no agency, no vitality of its own. As Foster and Clark (2016) observe, it was Alfred Schmidt (1970) in *The Concept of Nature in Marx* that gave birth to what became a commonplace interpretation that Marx (and also Engels) wanted to see nature placed under human techno-industrial dominion and that any 'new society is to benefit man alone'. As one of the Frankfurt School, his works smacks of the despair and pessimism that has been associated with the school, that essentially, we are all doomed to live in a Weberian iron cage with little hope of any form of future enchantment or future joy. Schmidt's critical voice has been joined since he was writing in the 1970s by deep ecologists keen to point out that Marxism was yet another variant of the industrial modernism that cared nothing beyond the needs of humans and was happy to pollute the planet. Like the supposed rupture between the young and mature Marx, tackled later in this chapter, we see another interpretation of Marx that has become an axiom, a taken-for-granted belief about Marx that does not stand the test of proper scrutiny.

I will spend time discussing Marx and nature. Why? First, Marx's supposed dismissal of nature and the environment has been a point of criticism over the years, as outlined earlier, and given the importance of nature within Marx's philosophy, such criticism, or rather misunderstandings, could undermine his theory of alienation. Second, as Dickens (2002) has discussed, humans are alienated from nature, and the loss for humanity that entails. For me, that alienation from nature is important given that wellbeing is a focus of this book. A plethora of material exists that clearly indicates that human wellbeing emerges from the environment and nature. One tranche of research on environment and wellbeing expounds that being in nature positively affects human wellbeing. Material on green and blue spaces (that is, parks, lakes and being by the seaside or coast) indicate that time spent away from concrete and tarmac can be good for wellbeing. Critical in research, such as that by Lachowycz and Jones (2013, 2014), is that simple physical activity, such as jogging, walking and swimming, is not what solely confers the wellbeing advantage. The relation is more complex. Wellbeing emerges from various relations with memory, identity and social interactions, but also the materiality and agency of nature. In researching why being near rivers improved wellbeing, Völker and Kistemann (2011) found that watching the flow of the River Rhine, the materiality of the vibrant moving water, and associations with it, created a sense of calm and tranquillity. While catching sight of a wild animal can also lead to positive consequences for wellbeing.

The benefits of nature, green and blue spaces, are however conditioned by the relations of capitalism and class. The wellbeing effects of green and blue spaces exist within a wider set of relations. Their presence alone is insufficient to overcome the effects of poverty and inequality. In the Scottish city of Glasgow, one of the most affluent areas of the city, Bearsden, and one of the most deprived, Drumchapel (colloquially, The Drum) both face onto Colquhoun Park.[2] It is a reasonably large green space laid out with football pitches, mature trees and play areas for children, offering many of the features that can make green space beneficial for wellbeing. But average life expectancy in affluent Bearsden is 80.5 for men and 83.5 for women, while in deprived Drumchapel it is 12 years less. It takes ten minutes to walk from one side to the other.

Nature in this context is what exists around, through and in humans. Its existence is fundamental for human survival. As such it is a creative relation and a core relation. Without nature there would be no humanity as we experience it today. This is a point that Marx brings home repeatedly in *Capital*, especially in the first volume, where one could read Marx as being some form of proto-ecologist (Foster 2000; see also Saito 2017, 2023). He refers to humans and nature living in a metabolic relationship with each other and of nature providing humanity with its first tools. Marx is also aware that what is nature and how humans make use of nature can appear to be very unnatural. Consider a mobile phone. It may give the surface appearance of being unnatural, made of out plastics and so on. Nature is present, however. Plastics are derived from oil and oil itself is a product of natural processes: the millennia-long decay and compression of countless creatures who existed in geologically ancient times. And at the heart of the mobile phone the main processor chip relies upon very distinct metals, the extraction of which relies upon the strip mining of ancient woodlands in Indonesia. So, in many respects, there is nothing artificial in the objects that humans produce, they are reconfigured nature, though nature reconfigured by both living and dead human labour.

How Marx understood humans' relationship with nature has been a source of debate and critique. He has been accused of advancing a productivist philosophy that places humanity at the centre of everything, in which nature is relegated to a passive resource that waits to be activated by human agency, and the consequences of human action, the damage to the ecosphere with all its biotic and abiotic elements, are of little interest to Marx. Human

---

[2]   If you are unfamiliar with these areas take a walk on Google Street View. You will see the park and the very stark contrast between Bearsden and Drumchapel.

interactions, in the epoch of the Capitalocene (Moore 2016), with nature are under increased focus in new strands of thinking concerning humans' place on the planet. A host of research reveals the damage to wellbeing that climate change and extreme weather cause for humans, other species and other matter. Both Marx and Engels were aware of how capital damaged ecosystems and the impact that industrialization has on nature. Here is Engels railing against the environmental degradation created by capitalist expansion:

> As individual capitalists are engaged in production and exchange for the sake of the immediate profit, only the nearest, most immediate results must first be taken into account. As long as the individual manufacturer or merchant sells a manufactured or purchased commodity with the usual coveted profit, he is satisfied and does not concern himself with what afterwards becomes of the commodity and its purchasers. The same thing applies to the natural effects of the same actions. What cared the Spanish planters in Cuba, who burned down forests on the slopes of the mountains and obtained from the ashes sufficient fertilizer for one generation of very highly profitable coffee trees—what cared they that the heavy tropical rainfall afterwards washed away the unprotected upper stratum of the soil, leaving behind only bare rock! In relation to nature, as to society, the present mode of production is predominantly concerned only about the immediate, the most tangible result. (Engels 1975: 17)

Marx also understood that capitalism came at a price for the environment:

> The 'essence' of the freshwater fish is the water of a river. But the latter ceases to be the 'essence' of the fish and is no longer a suitable medium of existence as soon as the river is made to serve industry, as soon as it is polluted by dyes and other waste products and navigated by steamboats, or as soon as its water is diverted into canals where simple drainage can deprive the fish of its medium of existence. (Marx and Engels 1976: 58–59)

Moore (2016) invites us to think about capitalism from a different perspective. He centres nature in a historical account of capitalism's genesis, and how the historical arrival of capitalism involved more than the reorganization and reordering not just of people but of vast swathes of the planet, non-human animals, plants and other matter. This history of capital runs against conventional historical narratives, which focus on the transformation of people, and the violent transfer of people from the countryside into the new manufactories of Manchester and Glasgow, which created the new subjectivity of the worker as opposed to the subjectivity of the rural serf or peasant (Reed 2016). Capitalism required more than human exploitation for it to become the dominant system it is today. It also needed to reorganize and alter all forms of planetary life and always was a multi-species process, as Moore insightfully notes. Capitalism exploited not just cheap human labour in the form of the emerging proletariat but also the cheap or free labour of nature, of insects, animals and plants alongside the transformation of the landscape of water systems, soils and minerals. In understanding that it is capitalism that is driving epochal changes in climate he advocates the use of Capitalocene instead of the more commonly used term of Anthropocene. The latter misses the point as to what is driving the damage to the planet. It is not humans per se that are creating climate change, but rather a particular economic form that has evolved over long periods of time that requires the destruction of natural matter for the creation of profit.

It can be established, therefore, that Marx and Engels were more than aware of what human activity could do to the environment and the increased damage that capitalism as a social and economic form did to ecosystems, and the importance of nature for human existence. That is a powerful comment to make in establishing that Marx was far from guilty of a simple one-sided productivist fallacy. However, that does not necessarily let him off the human-centred hook. Theories of nature, as found in neo-materialist and post-human discourses, offer more subtle and nuanced approaches, bringing to the fore the thingness and vitality of non-human matter. This body of work raises the point that matter possesses its own agency that operates with pre-human agency. A whole world of agency therefore operates beyond human interaction and independent of human activity and human agency. Marx is therefore accused of lacking a sophisticated understanding of nature. The recent work of Saito (2017) provides a useful counter in this regard. He makes the claim that we need to understand Marx's theory of metabolism if we are to understand, on one hand, how capitalism leads to environmental degradation and, on the other, how his ecological critics can be answered.

In Marx's theory of metabolism, as interpreted by Saito (2017), humans exist within and because of nature. One element in the multiple relations that make up being human is that humans are embodied creatures, as discussed earlier in relation to embodiment and in the core Marxist theory of labour power. They need food and water to survive, time to rest and recuperate, otherwise they simply die. That condition of needing nature is a condition of existence that all human societies have faced and will continue to face. It is an inescapable condition of being human: no nature, no humans. And the only source of food and water can be found in nature. That claim is not that controversial and still leaves the door open to charges of productivism: it is good to acknowledge the dependency of humans on nature, but that position still centres humanity.

The agency of matter, of nature and of other creatures that functions and operates external to human activity has been raised by neo-materialist and post-humanist writers in order to decentre humans as part of a wider project to theorize and include all forms of matter. Pollinating plants, for example, emit a blue, fluorescent light, a halo, that is not perceptible to humans but is visible to pollinator species such as bees. In fact, the blue light animates a frenzied response in the bees to seek out the flowers and collect pollen. The agency here is exercised by the plant as it seeks to produce more plants in a process that exists outside any involvement of humanity. The world is full of such interactions, a buzz of agency occurring second by second of which human agency is one form of agency.

Saito (2017) finds through a close reading of Marx that he was very much aware that nature and other forms of matter (or materials as he put it) possess what neo-materialist writers regard as agency, or 'thing power' as proposed by Bennett (2004). Critically, the agency of materials that humans use is vital in the pursuit of creating use-values and exchange value. The whole of Marx's economic theories, for Saito, understand that the material or matter being worked on by a human is not just a passive element in the labour process. It is one that possesses properties that pre-exist human interaction with it. Saito points to this extract from the section in *Capital* on the commodity as he builds his argument:

> When man engages in production, he can only proceed as nature does herself, i.e. he can only change the form of the materials. Furthermore, even in this work of modification he is constantly helped by natural forces. Labour is therefore not the only source of material wealth, i.e. of the use-values it produces. As William Petty says, labour is the father of material wealth, the earth is its mother. (Marx 1990: 133–134)

Nature is clearly here imbued with its own 'natural forces' that can only be modified and adapted by humans. A dialectic exists here between the agency of human labour and the agency of the material. What the material is capable of being when the material is transformed into use-value is determined not by what humans desire it to be but by the innate qualities of the material. The agency of the material is granted a place within this relation. Electric vehicles provide a useful example of the agency of matter within the production of a commodity. Nickel is an essential element within batteries for electric cars. It is a necessary component with the cathodes of a battery and its presence allows energy to be stored more densely and, therefore, more efficiently. Without nickel the whole of Tesla cars and Elon Musk's wealth, for example, may never have happened. The agency of nickel creates at first a use-value, the storage of electricity to power a vehicle, which in turn becomes an exchange value when it becomes, following the example, part of a Tesla car. By the way, despite electric cars' green gloss they come at an environmental cost. Remote locations and indigenous people are affected by the strip mining of the mineral, which results in disruption to indigenous communities and the destruction of vast swathes of land.

A metabolic and internally related dialectic is established between humans and nature. That relationship is further affected by human history and to what end the use-value is put. Each human historical epoch creates different use-values for what is created during the transformation of natural material. An historical example helps to illustrate this point.

The Latin American Muisca society, in its pre-colonial form, produced subtle and exquisite metal work using either gold, or a gold and copper alloy. They typically crafted flat plaques of highly stylized human figures cast using the lost wax technique, which produced highly intricate ornate pieces that involved very little postproduction work. In this set of relations in the creation of a gold figure the agency and natural forces of both the wax and metals are essential in the process of labour. Without them the figure could not be made. That point may seem stunningly obvious, but as Saito points out, many Marxists, such as Sohn-Reitl, deny the natural force of the materials that are part of labour. He considers them to be incidental and thus need not be considered. Remaining with the example the natural forces are critical. The malleability of the beeswax, which can be easily shaped into a variety of forms and models, makes possible the shape and detail of the figurine. The reflective bright surface of copper and gold further adds to what is happening because in the same moment as the agency of the matter functions a human symbolic order is animating and the human agency of creativity is enacted. The sheen of gold is representative of activity and of the Sun. The beeswax symbolizes fertility.

The finished object of labour for Muisca people did not possess an exchange value, as gold is understood today. They were certainly not intended to be a form of conspicuous consumption. The use of gold was purely symbolic and embedded within their belief system and did not represent wealth. Sometimes the gold objects were placed in religiously meaningful places, sacred caves and so on, and hidden from view.

Within the set of relations outlined here we can see different agencies and natural forces combining in the same moment. The act of labour may have been initiated by the human element but the object with its use-value cannot come into being without the pre-human agency and natural forces of the wax and gold. That example is located in a non-capitalist society. As Saito continues in his work, the historical arrival of capitalism alters that relationship between natural matter and humans. Nature becomes the raw stuff of capital where its ultimate exchange value is valued above all else, and the humans who transform nature become part of a process of exploitation of both humans and nature. What Marx can offer is an analysis of how humans exist within nature, and why and how human activity can lead to environmental degradation and the climate emergency, which affects all forms of matter on this planet. Humans do have an impact on the environment, and they do so due to their own nature as needing to survive on one level as part of their human nature. But something distinctive exists about the Capitalocene, and how it is an economic system that is ruining the planet, leading to extreme weather conditions, floods, heatwaves and travesties.

Towards other species alienation and why other creatures, too, must become free

Can alienation theory be extended to include other species, whether that be humans and non-human animals being alienated from each other, or that non-human animals are themselves alienated? I touched on animals in the preceding section on nature but did not consider them in any great depth. One commonly held assumption is that Marx is irreducibly anthropocentric with no regard for other species. After all, in one of the few passages in his work where he hints at what a post-capitalist society may be like, he revels in the time that will be made available for hunting, shooting and fishing. Other textual examples exist that could be read as indicative of Marx scorning the importance of animals, positing them as inferior and worthless entities.

Wilde (2000) provides a useful critical overview of the debate concerning the status of animals within Marx's writings. His main contention is that Marx, while far from being an ardent animal liberationist,[3] does not at any point dismiss the importance of animals. Marx instead draws attention to the *qualitative* differences between humans and animals. The main qualitative difference is that humans can produce tools that make other tools that change over generations. Limited evidence exists of animals ever achieving that same level of tool use. Yes, animal use tools and change over time is evident. Falótico et al (2019), for example, provide archaeological evidence of tool use and changes in tool use by capuchin monkeys in Brazil going back 3,000 years. The monkeys have used different forms of lithic (stone) tools to pound the shells of cashews to extract the nut. One variation in tool use occurred sometime between 2,400 years and 300 years ago, and another change in the last hundred years.

That is an amazing insight into how another species can change and adapt over time. However, think about how much humans have changed their tools and what they can produce in the same time frame. A nice

---

[3] Just for the record, I am an advocate of animal liberation. We should move away from animal-based food and definitely end unnecessary animal testing. I see the best way to achieve these ends lies in a post-capitalist society.

illustration is provided by two human constructions situated on a small hill in the Howe of Cromar in Aberdeenshire. Within a few metres of each other sit the 5,000-year-old Tomnaverie recumbent standing stone circle and a nuclear fallout monitoring post built in 1960 during the Cold War. It is a slightly longer arc of time than the 3,000 years mentioned for the capuchin monkeys but think about the tool development undertaken by humans in that timespan. The same species, humans, once used a variety of lithic and tools made from other materials to build the stone circle and in a few thousand years developed tools that could split the atom, with the potential to end the existence of multiple species. I would personally have preferred it if the development over that time had been more positive, but wars are always intrinsic to hierarchical societies. The point made here is that human tool development is on a different scale than that of animals. Yes, animals use tools, yes, they can make highly intricate structures, think of bees and the complexities of a hive, but it is discontinuous with what humans can achieve. By claiming that point I am not implying a superiority exists, just a difference.

It could also be argued that trying to diminish human uniqueness by arguing that non-animals have parallel capacities to humans is an anthropocentrism by the back door: a human characteristic is used to judge the values of other beings. We should instead accept differences exist and respect those differences, and as Wilde (2000: 49) states, human transition to a post-capitalist society needs to 'take sensitive and responsible control of the management of the interchange between human nature and non-human nature, including other animals'.

Wilde (2000: 47–48) is also critical of Benton (1993) and Elster (1985), both of whom have provided the intellectual yardage in casting Marx as a villain of species imperialism. The main charges Wilde makes against them is that they posit that humans are not as unique as Marx maintains. That point has been dealt with earlier. The other charge, and this is more applicable to Benton than Elster, is a misreading of Marx. One piece of evidence against Marx mobilized by Benton is that Marx makes explicitly derogatory remarks concerning animals. Benton claims that Marx regards non-human animals as primitive and often refers to the activities of non-human animals with a dismissive 'merely'. That evidence is easily refuted. Wilde draws attention to earlier translations from German into English of Marx, which did not accurately reflect what Marx wrote.

One useful example is the Moore and Aveling translation, which renders 'Wir haben es hier nicht mit den ersten tierartig instinktmassigen Formen der Arbeit zu tun' (Marx and Engels 1976: 192–193) as 'We are not now dealing with those primitive instinctive forms of labour that remind us of the mere animal' (Marx and Engels 1976: 187). As Wilde notes, the original German does not refer to either primitive or mere. A more accurate English phrasing is provided by Eden and Cedar Paul: 'those primitive and instinctive forms of labour which we share with other animals' (Wilde 2000: 48). The different translations are very different in their meaning. The first by Moore and Aveling is dismissive of animals while the second provided by Eden and Cedar Paul is quite different, pointing to commonalities between humans and animals.

We can, overall, state that charges against Marx regarding animals miss the mark. He is not, repeat not, what we would now think of as a deep ecologist or animal liberationist, but neither is he a species imperialist. Non-human animals occupy at worst a neutral space within his overall philosophy and at best that when humanity gains control over their history in a post-capitalist society then that transition is not complete without creating an equal relationship with nature.

A case can also be made, *pace* Dyer-Witheford (2009), that Marx's theory of species-being can be extended to include other species. If we centre labour within nature as an act that qualifies a being as human, then perhaps labour can act as a bridge to including other species too if we agree that something about labour is special and a qualification of exception or the granting of rights? In addition to the four main modalities, could species alienation come into play, where human and animal workers are alienated from each other and their work also subject to reification?

Humans encounter the products of other non-human animal species all the time, but, as with the objects produced by other humans, the subjectivity of that worker is not known, and the object appears as an entity in its own reified right. What are those products? Some are easy to identify, products like dairy and honey, which are derived from a particular animal, a cow or bee. Care must be taken to not just assume that since an animal can be identified no reification exists or alienation from other species. Humans are often presented with Disneyfied images of domesticated animals that are part of the production process, such as dairy cattle roaming over hillsides or anthropomorphic bees who are busy buzzing around their homely hive. Stanton (2021: 11) points to what she calls the 'happy farm' myth where animals are depicted in various media (think of the movie *Babe* about a pig) living happy lives in a romanticized old-fashioned bucolic farm, the charms of which are far removed from the brutal realities of contemporary capitalist factory farming.

How alienation theory could be applied to animals is provided by Stuart et al (2013) in their analysis of alienation and dairy cattle. While acknowledging that substantial differences exist between humans and non-human animals, and the latter are not involved in wage labour, dairy cattle are undoubtedly exploited within capitalist farming. They also exist within a set of social and economic relations defined by the logics of capitalism and become part of the labour process of producing a commodity (milk).

If we further acknowledge dairy cattle as sentient and suffering beings, then it is reasonable to see that alienation theory can be applied to other species.

Alienation, continuity and the epistemological break

Finally, an old issue that will never be fully resolved: did the mature Marx drop alienation theory? It is a thorny issue with passionate and compelling arguments mobilized by either side of the continuity debate. As Cowling (2006: 319) notes: 'Where alienation is concerned the older Marx has something to puzzle everyone.' While Dyer-Witheford (2004: 4) wearily concedes, '[t]he concept of species-being has thus been for some time caught in stand-off between humanist Marxists – who love it for its emancipatory élan – and structuralist Marxists – who scorn it for residual Hegelianism'.

It is Althusser who is responsible for making the claim that alienation theory plays no part in the mature and, what he terms, scientific works of Marx. He co-opts Bachelard's (1968) concept of the epistemological obstacle, where in the natural sciences various obstacles exist historically prior to science, such as opinion or general knowledge, and need to be overcome to allow a purer science to come into being. Althusser develops Bachelard's philosophy into his famous concept of the 'epistemological break', a theory similar to a Kuhnian paradigm shift, where one body of ideas and theories in science give way to a different body of ideas and theories (Arditi 2006). The humanism of the young Marx was therefore a necessary stage that Marx had to work through to arrive at his properly scientific theories, they were the initial footsteps he took, but they led him down a different path.

Althusser's (2005) whole project rests on his assertion that in 1845 a rupture and discontinuity occurred in Marx's thought. Either side of that year a different Marx exists, that bear no relationship to each other, an epistemological year zero, where Marx clears out and dispenses with the humanist follies of his youth. Marx's problematic shifts from a focus on human essence to a focus on the forces and relations of production, the bread and butter of historical materialism, or put more simply, away from a humanistic focus on human subjects to a scientific focus on social and economic structures. The early works, and especially the *Economic and Philosophic Manuscripts*, are not Marxism, but rather the work of an 'avantgarde Feuerbachian applying an ethical problematic to the understanding of human history' (Althusser 2005: 45). When Marx settled his account with Feuerbach and Hegel, in what Althusser claims to be the 'Works of the Break', then he settled his account with alienation too. Any recourse to alienation or analysis of capitalism that involved human essence required rejection from the Marxist canon with full attention instead applied to understanding the structures of society. Marxism, for Althusser, should be rigorous and scientific, and devoid of any metaphysical infusions and distractions. The rupture therefore has consequences for the status and place of alienation theory within Marxism as a whole. For Althusser, alienation was infected by not just residual humanism but too much of Feuerbach's particular version of humanism. Throughout his writings, Althusser leaves the reader in no doubt about his contempt for humanism or alienation. He clearly states the target of his work as 'these humanist ravings, these feeble dissertations on liberty, labour or alienation' (Althusser 1975).

Althusser's Marxism developed in reaction to the humanist Marxism of the times, but also against Stalinist orthodoxy. Looking back at the 1960s, a time celebrated and remembered for its radicalism, it needs to be recalled that many on the left, especially those who were members of various Western European communist parties, were still in thrall to the state capitalism and Stalinism of Soviet Russia. National communist parties followed the party line from Moscow, the ultimate aim of Moscow was not the spread of internationalism and the proletariat revolution, but to advance global-political ambitions of state capitalist Russia in the *Realpolitik* of the Cold War. Althusser's intervention was to try to steer the French Communist Party (Parti Communiste Français) away from Stalinism and Moscow by attacking their Stalinist standpoint. He saw his emphasis on the structural elements of Marxism as vital in challenging the personality cult of Stalin, and that Stalin was somehow the unique revolutionary subject capable of sweeping away capitalism.

Lukács' work is highlighted as particularly deficient by Althusser for his 'fashionable theory of "reification"' (Althusser 1969).[4] Althusser's main objection is the emphasis on the subject within humanism, that the knowing and aware subject can rise up and overthrow capitalism once a certain level of class consciousness is attained. In Lukács' Marxism, the working class is restrained from revolutionary activity by the reification of commodity fetishism in capitalist society. Instead of recognizing the existence other social agents with whom they share the commonality of exploitation within the capitalist system, workers see objects, thus obscuring the totality in which they exist. All that is necessary for revolution to occur is for workers to cast off any false consciousness, see through that veil and grasp the totality. One immediate weakness with Lukács is the power inhered in the structures of capitalism is underdeveloped and he can lapse into a form of reductionism.

---

[4] I do not want to draw out the merits and demerits of Althusser or Lukács as that can be found elsewhere (for commentaries, see Callinicos 1976 and Rees 1998), and would be a digression from the main task of this section of answering the question of the continuity of alienation in Marxism. But I feel it is useful to touch on why Althusser drew attention to the epistemological break, and the context in which he was writing. There is much in Althusser's writing that is useful, but my focus here is dealing with a critique that is constantly raised against alienation studies.

Althusser sought to correct the privileging of the subject in Lukács, and in wider humanist versions of Marxism, by claiming that the mature Marx had no truck with humanism and that it is only by focusing on the structures of society that we can move to a scientific and, more importantly, revolutionary analysis. One downside of Althusser's emphasis on structures was that humans disappear, passive entities waiting to be interpellated, called into being, by social structures, like a non-player character waiting to be activated in a scene of a game.

It does seem odd that while his overbearing structuralism no longer finds favour and has few proponents today, that his one legacy is the assumption that he was correct in arguing for the total disappearance of the earlier work of Marx. His work was not greeted with universal acclaim at the time and questions can be raised about Althusser's overall contribution to Marxism. Those who did adopt an Althusserian perspective in their academic and political careers, such as Hindess and Hirst (1975), eventually came to question the supposed scientificity of Althusser, his defining character. They found that Althusser was guilty of the Western metaphysics he sought to purge from Marxism and that his theory of ideology was a disguised form of functionalism (Elliott 1987). In the case of Hirst (1976) he had said goodbye to Althusser by the late 1970s, with Hirst slipping into abrupt changes in political and intellectual direction and finding a home in reformist politics. Other followers of Althusser crossed the floor to post-structuralism. One can then ask the question: if Althusser's version of Marxism was so correct and scientific why did its influence wane so quickly? As Zoubir (2018) states, and what I was attempting to indicate by sketching out the times in which Althusser was writing, Althusser's intervention was more out of what he saw as political necessity. The humanism of Marxism of that time he felt did not provide the sufficient theoretical bedrock on which to build revolution. That was his target, and alienation theory was collateral damage in that political project.

A methodological flaw also exists within the epistemological break thesis, which further substantiates my point. As I said earlier, Althusser calls on Bachelard's philosophy of science and applies it to Marxism. There is a problem. In Bachelard's philosophy of science it is taken as read that science was successful in sweeping away its pre-history and establishing itself in the scientific present. To that end, Bachelard does not offer, as O'Boyle and McDonough (2016) note, a mechanism to accurately judge the extent and success of a supposed rupture. That may be not so difficult for science for Bachelard as he thought it was obvious that science had escaped its historical obstacles. However, Althusser never advances any method by which anyone can judge that Marxism had become more scientific.

How strong is Althusser's case? Althusser did not support his contention of an epistemological break very well according to Carver (2008). The exact date of when the rupture occurs moves and shifts, 'until the point at which Marx himself no longer seemed to live up to his own "scientific" and "anti-philosophical ideal"' (Carver 2008: np). Elliott (1987) notes that by Althusser's own admission, in his later work, only two pieces by Marx meet the criteria for scientific purity as being unsullied by Feuerbach or Hegel. One of which was 'Marginal Notes on Adolph Wagner's *Lehrbuch der Politischen Ökonomie*', written in 1881–1882 shortly before Marx's death in 1883, which pushes the date of the rupture pretty close to the final days of Marx himself.

Then there is the tortured recommendations that Althusser gave in reading Marx. The correct place to begin reading *Capital*, averred Althusser, was not the opening pages where the commodity is studied as a gateway into the inner workings of capitalism. Those passage still retain, in the discission of commodity fetishism, the taint of humanism. Better to start with Part II on 'The Transformation of Money into Capital', which is more scientific in his analysis.

Various writers have come down on either side of the debate and, returning to Cowling, it is a hard call to make. It all depends on what counts as admissible evidence in the case for or against a continuity in Marx, for example, which texts provide proof one way or the other. Those supporting the continuity thesis point to the *Grundrisse* to win their case, a tactic employed by Mészáros (1975), where indeed multiple references to alienation can be found. Cowling cites Lewis (1972), who has painstakingly counted over 300 references to alienation in the *Grundrisse*. Case closed it would seem. But the status of *Grundrisse* for Cowling may undermine this otherwise telling evidence. The *Grundrisse* was Marx's notes and preparatory draft for *Capital*. It was not the finished article. If alienation, as per the *Economic and Philosophic Manuscripts* or a more sophisticated version of it, was an important part of his mature thought then it would have been included. However, that requires jettisoning *Grundrisse*, with all the rich insights and fertile material that it has provided over the years. It is also a matter of debate what constitutes the finality of Marx's thought. After all, what we find as the published works are subject to Engels' curation of what he thought was best to be published and the editorial decisions he made. Also, as K.B. Anderson (2016) brought to the fore, recent research into the notebooks of the older Marx indicate further development of his thought in terms of humanity's relationship with the environment and a shift towards a more nuanced understanding of colonialism.

My perspective on the existence of alienation in the later works of Marx follows that of Carver (2008) and Zoubir (2018), which runs as follows. Marx's work develops and changes over time and cannot always be seen as a continuous project, but it is hard to sustain that the discontinuity means that all the younger aspects of Marxism need to be dismissed.

Alienation persists in the writings of the older Marx, but it does so in a way that is different from the *Economic and Philosophic Manuscripts*. Marx was dealing at that point with the failings of his main influences, Hegel and Feuerbach. Alienation and human nature therefore play a central role in the *Economic and Philosophical Manuscripts*. Marx was always expanded and developing his theories and analysis. As he develops, his interest turns to analysing political economy in greater depth. Hence, the focus of his later work is identifying the core relations of capital, and they are therefore to the fore in his exposition (Rosdolsky 1992). That observation, though, does not entail that he dispenses with or rejects alienation. It becomes a lesser part of his analysis, but it is still prevalent and present when he wants to turn to how the structures of capital affect workers, humanity and nature. Overall, a theory of alienation can be created from across Marx's writings. What the later material provides is a clearer analysis of the objective conditions in which human subjectivity becomes estranged and how the commodification of humanity and reification of what workers produce leads to poor wellbeing and the reduction of what humans are capable of. Sève (1978) takes up this point in his application of Marxist theory to psychology.

As a contemporary of Althusser, Sève witnessed the debates and the wrangling surrounding humanist versus scientific readings of Marx. He finds both sides unsatisfactory, positing incomplete interpretations of Marx that overemphasize one element over the other. Though he is very clear that Marx never did abandon his humanism, he just developed further with his scientific analysis of capitalism and how that human nature takes a historical form. To that end, Sève puts forward a 'scientific humanism' 'as the theory of the contradictions and conditions of the historical flowering of individuals. And of the necessary advent of what Marx calls the fully developed individual in communist society' (Séve 1978: 125). One implication of Sève's scientific humanism requires understanding humans in concrete historical reality, how their lives are experienced amid the structures of capitalism. My case study in Chapter 4 hopefully provides an example of what that may involve.

Conclusion

Criticism of Marx rests on taken-for-granted assumptions about what he said. For example, that Marx advanced a form of species imperialism that devalues nature, or that a clean break exists between the young and mature Marx. What I have presented in this chapter hopefully unsettles those assumptions. That position does not however entail that the opposite is true, that Marx was an out-and-out ecologist or that alienation is a central theme throughout all phases of his life. The reality is much more complex, with plenty of gaps and contradictions evident in what he wrote. I have drawn on authors who have tried to tease out and provide more nuanced readings of Marx, that can provide a useful alternative to the more unwarranted readings that present an incorrect and misleading interpretation.

Chapter 3 argues for how alienation theory can assist in analysing and understanding health and wellbeing.

3

Alienation and Wellbeing

Introduction

Engels provided one of the strongest and most famous indictments in the Marxist canon of capitalism and the suffering it causes with his accusation against the bourgeoise that they commit 'social murder':

> When one individual inflicts bodily injury upon another such that death results, we call the deed manslaughter; when the assailant knew in advance that the injury would be fatal, we call his deed murder. But when society places hundreds of proletarians in such a position that they inevitably meet a too early and an unnatural death, one which is quite as much a death by violence as that by the sword or bullet; when it deprives thousands of the necessaries of life, places them under conditions in which they cannot live – forces them, through the strong arm of the law, to remain in such conditions until that death ensues which is the inevitable consequence – knows that these thousands of victims must perish, and yet permits these conditions to remain, its deed is murder just as surely as the deed of the single individual; disguised, malicious murder, murder against which none can defend himself, which does not seem what it is, because no man sees the murderer, because the death of the victim seems a natural one, since the offence is more one of omission than of commission. But murder it remains. (Engels 1993: 106)

Engels is drawing attention to how the avoidable deaths of tens of thousands of people are made invisible by what McGarvey (2023) would today call the social distance between the murdered and the murderer. The assailant in a social murder is always absent from the scene of the crime. The relations of capital, between worker and bourgeoisie, leave no fingerprints, nor samples of DNA that can identify a perpetrator. The insightfulness of Engels lies in his assertion that the harm capitalism creates is assumed to be, as he says, natural, with the implication that no individual nor social class of people bear any responsibility. Poor health and wellbeing are waived away as plain bad luck, or, within the responsibilization discourses of neoliberalism, poor wellbeing is the result of an individual making bad choices about their health and wellbeing – perhaps deciding to smoke too much or indulging in too many high-fat foods. As Medvedyuk et al (2021) observe, a re-emergence of the term of social murder has reappeared in discussions of tragic events and the persistence of increasing health inequalities. Two recent examples of its application in the United Kingdom are the COVID-19 pandemic, where the botched handling of the crisis by the Conservative government led to thousands of early and unnecessary deaths, and the horror of Grenfell Tower where 72 working-class people and people of colour died after years-long protestations concerning fire safety were ignored by the local Conservative council.

The opioid crisis in the United States is another example of social murder: 136 people die each day due to an opioid overdose, and between the years 1999 and 2019 just over 500,000 Americans died due to an opioid overdose (CDC 2022). From 2013 onwards the majority of these deaths are attributable to synthetic opioids manufactured by large American pharmaceutical corporations. A considerable, mainly clinical or psychological, literature exists attempting to explain what is going on and turns on the conclusion that social isolation, or some form of lack of connectedness with other people, is to blame. Christie (2021), for example, makes a case that social isolation is behind the opioid crisis, and that humans are hard-wired to be social. Drawing on a range of studies and findings from a variety of fields she finds that if social connectedness is removed then negative consequences follow. She claims that opioids help in filling the void that a lack of contact can create. Case and Deaton (2020) refer to these high rates of mortality as 'deaths of despair', where people's lives are wiped out due to deeper structural realignments of American capitalism. Wages have flatlined since the 1970s, well paid and stable employment in manufacturing has gone. Industries, such as steel, are offshored to China, leaving behind a rustbelt in states such as Appalachia and the poorer parts of the American eastern seaboard. This social murder is, for me, alienation writ large. A sense of purpose, the connections between people and some form of structure that factory life gave, has been wiped out and replaced with nothing, except for the aggressive marketing of opioids by large pharmaceutical companies – a return to opium is the religion of the masses, in that a chemical provides solace in the face of the destructiveness of capitalism.

We can turn to the visible tragedies of capitalism, like those just mentioned, as evidence of the suffering that capitalism causes, but it is also the invisibilized nature of alienation's effect on wellbeing that needs to be brought out into the open. The events such as the cases mentioned here need to be recognized as failures of capitalism and the suffering it causes. But alienation is also insidious in its effects on wellbeing, passing unnoticed or normalized into everyday life. Alienation is part of the 'hidden injuries of class', as Sennett and Cobb (1972) put it, or the objective violence, which Žižek (2008) claims is inherent within the daily machinations of capitalist society, which passes unrecognized as violence. The objective violence of alienation is the slow grind of working and living in a society structured around a lack of control, no outlet for self-realization and being fragmented and isolated from other people, or othered and stigmatized as being unworthy of recognition. Alienation takes place in the arteries, the nervous systems, the heart tissue and the cells of workers.

The rest of this chapter explores how alienation affects wellbeing, how it gets under the skin, and how Marxism understands wellbeing. It draws on the previous chapters, moving towards an understanding of wellbeing grounded in a Marxist materialism. In doing so, critiques are made of other wellbeing theories alongside an attempt to understand the dialectical relationships between wellbeing, humans, their emotions and their bodies.

I want to pause to first to sketch out a few critical points concerning health for any reader unfamiliar with the wider medical sociology literature on health inequalities. The vast corpus of research and theorization within medical sociology has made one outstanding contribution to both the discipline of sociology, and to wider knowledge concerning health and wellbeing: human health and wellbeing are complex, and much more than simply the function of biological processes or neoliberal deflection strategies that health and wellbeing are reducible to lifestyle and risk factors. What medical sociology reveals about health and wellbeing is the vital, if not central, role of the social. Wider social relations involving class, gender and ethnicity and so on mediate and condition health and wellbeing. And when the so-called risk factors such as smoking and diet are cited as causes of poor health they too are enmeshed in a wide assemblage of social relations. These relations also take into account economics, culture, history and, as neo-materialist writers point out, other forms of matter. The vast output of research on ethnicity and health, for example, reveals that it is context-specific racism that effects the health and wellbeing of racialized minorities (for examples of this research, see Williams et al 2019; Krieger 2020; Nazroo et al 2020) other than reference to lifestyle or diet. Inherent within this body of work is that racism emerges out of a long and brutal historical past of enslavement and colonialism that shapes the existence, societal and economic relations of people of colour today. It is structural racism that is the main risk factor for the wellbeing of people of colour rather than choices that individual people of colour make.

Understanding human health and wellbeing therefore requires the engagement of the sociological imagination to think beyond the familiar ideologies and discourses of health and wellbeing, which basically posit an individuated model of personal responsibility and personal choice. Human health and wellbeing exists within a complex set of relationships: how a society is organized, how relations of power are ordered and structured, and how the relations of material, cultural, economic and cultural resources can be accessed. A flow exists between these relations and the bodies, the minds and the emotions of social agents which, for many, result in poor health and poor wellbeing. The focus should rather be on how individuals and communities are shaped and influenced by power and structural relations rather than on their individual behaviours, the latter focus forming the default position of much public health policies or right-wing discourses of health and wellbeing.

What is wellbeing?

Huppert (2014) notes that the deep conceptual roots of wellbeing can be traced back to classical Greece and the philosophy of Aristippus and Aristotle, who both in their own ways attempted to understand what it means to lead a good and happy life. The current body of material on wellbeing stems mainly from the work of psychologists such as Seligman (2002, 2008; Seligman and Csikszentmihalyi 2000), a key and founding figure in the 'positive psychology' school, who has attempted to outline how individuals can attain authentic happiness. For Seligman (2002: 5), wellbeing is concerned with 'positive emotion, engagement, purpose, positive relationships, positive accomplishment'. Economics has also made significant contributions to the understanding of wellbeing. The work of Oswald (Clark and Oswald 1994, 1996; Oswald 1997), in particular, paving the way for that discipline to outline relations between issues such as unemployment, income, economic performance and happiness. There has been growing interest from other disciplines such as sociology, which has emphasized the social contexts of wellbeing, highlighting that wellbeing is wider than individual psychology. Though not much appears in the sociological literature concerning wellbeing up until the early part of this century (Cronin de Chavez et al 2005) a considerable distance has been travelled since then. Wainwright and Calnan (2011), for example, have argued for a shift away from models of health that, despite stated aims at being holistic, tend to focus on negative aspects of health towards perspectives on wellbeing that are truly encompassing of the many dimensions of human existence.

Wilkinson and Pickett (2010) have provided one of the most well-known pieces on wellbeing that places wellbeing into a wider social context. Their social-epidemiological research has indicated that for high-income nations overall societal wellbeing is affected by income inequalities. The basic tenet of their thesis holds that the greater the income inequality within a country, then the worse that country's wellbeing on a variety of, but not all, fronts will be. Their work has focused on health where they identify that more equal societies (for example, the Nordic nations and Japan) exhibit higher life expectancy than less equal countries such as the United Kingdom and the United States. The overall equality of a nation appears in their research to exert more of an effect on life expectancy than absolute income differences between nations. The power of equality can mean that poorer nations can exhibit a better life expectancy than wealthier ones. Average income in Chile is well behind that of the United States, but the average Chilean life expectancy is 1.4 years more than their northern American neighbours. In addition to health, a number of other aspects of wellbeing can be correlated to income inequality. Wilkinson and Pickett posit that countries with high income inequality can also experience higher levels of emotional distress, lower levels of trust, and worse problems with alcohol and other substances.

The disciplinary diversity of the roots apparent in the wellbeing literature make it conceptually heterodox with no single agreed definition of wellbeing. Ryan and Deci (2001) note two broad traditions existing within the literature on wellbeing. The first is hedonic, where the emphasis falls on subjective wellbeing with a narrow focus on the happiness and pleasure of an individual. The aim here is to maximize happiness and to dispense with negative feelings as and when they arise. Wellbeing literature that is influenced by this approach is operationalized by subjective wellbeing measures that attempt to assess levels of happiness experienced by an individual that are measurable by life satisfaction, the presence of positive mood and the absence of negative mood (Deci and Ryan 2008). Kahneman et al (1999: ix) provide one of the key texts in this tranche of literature. Their edited collection begins with a statement that captures the essence of the hedonic approach: 'Hedonic psychology ... is the study of what makes experiences and life pleasant or unpleasant. It is concerned with feelings of pleasure and pain, of interest and boredom, of joy and sorrow, and of satisfaction and dissatisfaction'.

The second approach is *eudaimonic*, which encompasses a wider and broader of vision of wellbeing. It is Aristotle (2004) who originated the concept of *eudaimonia*, mainly found in his *Nicomachean Ethics*, where he outlines what it is to lead a good life and to be happy. For Aristotle, achieving happiness is a life-long task where one needs to go beyond oneself, reach out to others and find meaning in what one does. Doing so may require that the individual forgoes short-term pleasure and happiness in pursuit of a longer-term deeper sense of self. The focus in the wellbeing literature that stands in this tradition therefore falls not just on passing emotional states of happiness and enjoyment, on feeling good as opposed to experiencing pain or sadness, but on deeper moments of self-realization and self-confirmation, where life is a project that concerns itself with engaging in meaningful activity and meaningful endeavours (Steger et al 2008). By engaging in those meaningful activities and endeavours one can access the core aspects of self and feel complete in what one what does. Crucially in the *eudaimonic* approach to wellbeing negative states are not avoided but can be accepted if they are necessary to gaining a fuller life.

Despite the differences in the two approaches, it is the common emphasis on developing, maintaining and creating a positive improvement (if not a lifting of the individual above their everyday life) that marks out many of the discourses on wellbeing. In the introduction to their edited collection on wellbeing, Haworth and Hart capture the main thrusts of the wider literature on wellbeing as follows:

[Wellbeing is] viewed variously as happiness, satisfaction, enjoyment, contentment; and engagement and fulfilment, or a combination of these, and other hedonic and eudaimonic factors. Wellbeing is also viewed as a process, something we do together and as sense-making rather than just a state of being. It is acknowledged that in life as a whole there will be periods of ill-being, and that these may add to the richness of life. It has also been recognised that wellbeing and environment are intimately interconnected. Certainly, wellbeing is seen to be complex and multifaceted and may take different forms. (Haworth and Hart 2012: 1)

Many criticisms exist of how wellbeing is theorized and the forms that wellbeing practice take in societies. The emphasis on happiness and on constantly performing a positive emotionality has been criticized by Williams (2000), who claims that this emphasis produces a false emotional self, a self subject to a process of what he terms 'Disneyfication', where all is wonderful, and all is optimistic. The end result is to negate and obliterate what he sees as the natural embodied emotions whose unpredictable rhythms do not easily fit the neat order of rational late-modernity. Carlisle et al (2009) in a similar vein upbraids the moves to wellbeing as sometimes lapsing into North American cultural norms (a 'Californication' of emotions).

One would probably expect that Marxism would not hold any sway with many popular trends in wellbeing, especially as certain elements, such as Goleman's (1996) Emotional Intelligence thesis, can be criticized as seeking to render a workplace emotionality that is compliant with the needs of the new managerialism (Hughes 2003), or criticizing discourses of wellbeing as yet another one of neoliberalism's individualizing impulses where it is the responsibility of the individual to create their own wellbeing mediated through consumerism regardless of social context (Sointu 2005; Horrocks and Johnson 2014). Mindfulness has become a popular technique to improve wellbeing. Its basic premise turns on being present in the moment and instead of fretting on the issues that are troubling you, focus should be on the immediacy of surroundings, thought, feelings and sensations being experienced in the here and now. Williams and Kuyken (2012) are bullish in their support for mindfulness, claiming that it can lead to reductions in episodes of depression, while Coelho et al (2013) have disputed its efficacy and evidential base. Indeed, as Walsh (2016) states, '[c]ritiques of mindfulness have now become so popular that they compete for the public's attention alongside regular reports of mindfulness' purported benefits'. My dispute with mindfulness is similar to what has been already said about Goleman and emotional intelligence. Mindfulness is yet another individuated approach to dealing with the emotional problems of capitalist modernity. Centre stage in mindfulness is the lone social agent focusing on their negative emotions, anything more than the immediate causes of which are elided or deemed beyond the remit of the approach. This approach is an example of Fisher's capitalist realism, where negative emotional states are privatized, and the solutions placed on the shoulders of individuals. The powerful social relationships that create the emotional states in the first place are let off the hook. It is an acceptance that no other form of social relationships is possible. Mindfulness can also be classed as a technology of self within neoliberalism. It is a retreat into the scented-candle meditative bunker of escapism, pushing back the brutal logics of capitalism with a yoga mat, or a technique for the neoliberal entrepreneurial subject to sharpen their self before joining battle in the marketplace.

Those points aside, there is much of interest (albeit critically) in the literature on wellbeing for Marxism: after all, the ultimate aim of Marx was to create a society where human self-realization, self-actualization and universal wellbeing are the goal of that society rather than the valorization of profit. As Marx and Engels (2015: 19) make clear in the *Communist Manifesto* a communist society is 'an association in which the free development of each is the condition for the free development of all'. That pithy dictum of Marx and Engels could be construed as a basis of Marxist understanding of wellbeing. We have already seen in the sections that discussed Marx's philosophical anthropology, especially in relation to Geras' (1985) meditations on a Marxian theory of human nature, what his understanding of wellbeing would be. A summary is provided here:

1. Humans experience wellbeing when they can exercise their innate creativity to alter the natural/social world around them for their mutual improvement.
2. Humans experience wellbeing when they can exercise control and autonomy in how and when they labour, giving free reign to the creativity identified in (1).

3. Humans experience wellbeing when cooperating and working with other humans. It is through contact with others that they can best realize (1) and (2).

4. Humans can only experience continual wellbeing in a particular social form. That social form is communist society where social relations and social structures of equality allow and support (1), (2) and (3).

As point 4 highlights, one absolute and crucial caveat must be entered when discussing Marx and wellbeing: that capitalist society cannot deliver wellbeing as it alienates social agents from the actual means of the ways in which that wellbeing can be achieved (Wood 2004). Marx does make frequent reference to what we would now term wellbeing. Notable and important is that wellbeing appears as an element within his discussions and analysis of capitalism generally, and alienation in particular. In the *Economic and Philosophic Manuscripts*, for example, Marx makes frequent association between alienation and poor wellbeing, as the following passage indicates:

> This relation is the relation of the worker to his own activity as an alien activity not belonging to him; it is activity as suffering, strength as weakness, begetting as emasculating, the worker's own physical and mental energy, his personal life – for what is life but activity? – as an activity which is turned against him, independent of him and not belonging to him. (Marx 1977: 65–66)

Marx's discussion of how capitalism influences wellbeing in his later work is mainly concentrated in chapters 10, 15 and 25 of *Capital I*. It sometimes consists of Marx's own analysis but is frequently based on secondary data drawn from various reports, and includes reference to 'potters' asthma … scrofula, pneumonia, phthisis, bronchitis and asthma' (Marx 1990: 355), or 'phthisis, bronchitis, irregularity of uterine functions, hysteria in its most aggravate forms and rheumatism' (Marx 1990: 410). In all cases where health problems are discussed it is in the context of exploitative and alienative working conditions and relationships, with the passages and chapters that centre on factory conditions providing the clearest examples. All four modes of alienation are evident. The most common mode that Marx alludes to is other-human alienation: the most cogent examples are the decisions of factory owners to extend working hours to punishing levels and the consequences that increase has for the workers' health.

The closely allied modes of process alienation and product alienation are evident in the descriptions of how the actual work is organized with no input from the workers as to that organization, and the primacy of what is being produced over the health of the worker. Finally, human–nature alienation is present in the various comments that Marx makes regarding how workers' potential, self-realization and species-being through labour is negated by capitalism. The following passage captures this synergy between alienative conditions, in this case the fragmentation of the labour process, and health:

> Some crippling of body and mind is inseparable even from the division of labour in society as a whole. However, since manufacture carries this social separation of branches of labour much further, and also, by its peculiar division, attacks the individual at the very roots of his life, it is the first system to provide the materials and the impetus for industrial pathology. (Marx 1990: 484)

The clearest example of Marx's interweaving of alienation and wellbeing can be found in the following passage from *Capital I* (the part IV that Marx refers to includes chapters 15 and 25 mentioned earlier):

> We saw in Part IV, when analysing the production of relative surplus-value, that within the capitalist system all methods for raising the social productivity of labour are put into effect at the cost of the individual worker; that all means for the development of production undergo a dialectical inversion so that they become means of domination and exploitation of the producers; they distort the worker into a fragment of a man, they degrade him to the level of an appendage of a machine, they destroy the actual content of his labour by turning it into a torment; they alienate *entfremden* from him the intellectual potentialities of the labour process ... they transform his life-time into working-time, and drag his wife and child beneath the wheels of the juggernaut of capital. But all methods for the production of surplus-value are at the same time methods of accumulation, and every extension of accumulation becomes, conversely, a means for the development of those methods. ... Accumulation of wealth at one pole is, therefore, at the same time accumulation of misery, the torment of labour, slavery, ignorance, brutalisation and moral degradation at the opposite pole, i.e. on the side of the class that produces its own product as capital. (Marx 1990: 798–799, emphasis added)

As a passage it would not seem misplaced in the *Economic and Philosophic Manuscripts* of the young Marx. What is most notable is Marx summarizing what he believes to be his core message from one of the most significant sections of *Capital I*: it is in part economic, dealing with surplus value, but its main focus is on the simultaneous alienation and damage to the worker, resulting in, 'misery, torment ... slavery, ignorance, brutalisation and moral degradation'.

The constant fusion of alienation and suffering has been noted by several others. For example, Wilkinson in his meditations on social suffering notes that:

> Marx displays a tendency to conceptualize the dynamics of the social body and the physical body as one; the 'subjective' experience of suffering is at the same time an expression of a society in pain, and it is only by addressing the social constituents of this experience that some manner of personal healing can take place. (Wilkinson 2004: 54)

Similar comments are provided by Merrifield (1999). He focuses on the relationship between suffering and alienation in Marx's writing, and how, for Marx, suffering is not the abstract idealist suffering proposed by Hegel but one that occurs in the bodies and minds of very real flesh-and-blood human beings. As insightful as these observations are, the full implications for a Marxist understanding of wellbeing have not been fully developed nor appreciated. The basic message is that alienation and negative physical and mental wellbeing share the same ontological reality: they are one and the same.

Wellbeing is therefore crucial to a study of alienation, as Wood makes clear that alienation is the negation of wellbeing:

> Marx often speaks of alienated life as one in which the human beings fail to 'affirm' (*bejahen*), 'confirm' (*bestätigen*), or 'actualise' (*verwirklichen*) themselves. A human life which is self-affirming, self-confirming and self-actualising is a meaningful life; a self which affirms, confirms and actualises itself is a self which has worth, and recognises the worth it has. (Wood 2004: 21)

This passage from Wood additionally points to a deeper philosophical connection with Marx and current concerns with wellbeing: both share the common influence of Aristotle. We saw earlier that current wellbeing discourses draw from Aristotle's concept of the *eudaimonia*, as does much of the ethical basis of Marxism that guides Marx's writings on alienation and capitalism (Carpenter 2010).

Any discussion of Aristotle and wellbeing brings me into dialogue with Nussbaum and her influential and well-known Aristotelian capabilities approach. I am not about to dismiss what Nussbaum says out of hand on the trite grounds of her being a liberal-individualist as it might be expected. Her ideas and scholarship are well argued and provocative. She is also fully cognisant of the challenges that introducing her capabilities approach into social policy entail. To that end, I feel her ideas are that of a radical reformist, who raises very important questions for governments and wider civil society.

73

I have already called on her work to support the defence of some form of limited essentialism in Chapter 2. But, more than that, a distinct influence of Marx pervades her theories and ideas more than might be expected. She frequently – and favourably – cites Marx (Nussbaum 2000, 2006), and has contributed to an edited collection on Marx and Aristotle, where she draws attention to the overlaps between Marx, Aristotle and her ideas (Nussbaum 1997). It is the humanist problematic of the young Marx on which she draws. At times her language could easily sit inside the *Economic and Philosophic Manuscripts*: 'What this approach is after is a society in which individuals are treated as each worthy of regard, and in which each has been put in a position to live really humanly' (Nussbaum 2000: 231).

Nussbaum's (2000, 2006) project is to identify capabilities that, because of their deliberate vagueness, can be of universal and global appeal and thereby act as the basis of global justice. Throughout her work the following capabilities, or human potentials, serve as the basis for what she understands as the good life:

1. *Life.* Being able to lead a full life.
2. *Bodily Health.* Being able to have good health.
3. *Bodily Integrity.* Being able to have physical security, sexual satisfaction, and choice about reproduction.
4. *Senses, Imagination, and Thought.* Being able to use the senses in a truly human way through education and guarantees of free expression.
5. *Emotions.* Being able to develop our emotions of love, grieving, longing and gratitude.
6. *Practical Reason.* Being able to form a conception of the good and to plan one's own life.
7. *Affiliation.* Being able to live with and for others. Being free from discrimination on the basis of race, sex, sexual orientation, ethnicity, caste, religion or national origin.
8. *Other Species.* Being able to live with concern for animals, plants, and the world of nature.
9. *Play.* Being able to laugh and play.
10. *Control over One's Environment.* Being able to participate politically, being able to hold property on an equal basis with others, and being able to work with meaningful relationships of recognition with other workers.

As Wilde (2011: 31) observes, points 6 and 7 on practical reason and affiliation are the building blocks for her whole project. With affiliation she is recalling Aristotle's *zoon politikon* that humans need each other, that humans are naturally social, a point of convergence with Marx and a point that prevents her from slipping into a reductive individualism. None of these points are wrong, nor is there much there I would argue against from a Marxist perspective. The tenth objective concerning the capacity to engage with 'meaningful relationships of recognition with other workers' is particularly welcome. The inclusion of other species is also welcome, given the earlier discussions of the openness of human species-being to incorporate other species and to recognize that alienation can exist in non-human animals too. It is very similar to the four-point summary of Marxism and wellbeing I provided earlier in this chapter. It is also similar to what Geras, who we encountered in Chapter 2, identified across Marx's writing. Such similarities are unsurprising considering their common Aristotelian influences. In fact, Nussbaum provides an account of capabilities that can be used to further flesh out a theory of alienation.

It is in how Nussbaum anticipates the means and mechanisms through which capacities can be enacted and realized that is problematic. The wider relations of capital require the prevention of the potentials and capabilities of social agents to flourish in order to maintain the valorization of profit. I agree with Wilde (2011) that if we accept a humanism in Marx then we are compelled to be constructive critics of Nussbaum. The criticism is that her Marx is one-sided and only limited to the positive aspects of what Marx discussed in the *Economic and Philosophic Manuscripts*. It is the humanist problematic of the young Marx as outlined in the *Economic and Philosophic Manuscripts*, but not the so-called scientific problematic of the older Marx with its clear analysis of the relations of production and the logics of capitalism.

Nussbaum outlines ten principles that offer the potential to promote the better life and create unfettered human flourishing that she advocates in her capabilities approach. The principles mainly rely on two modal verbs, 'should' and 'must', with their intrinsic expression of *possibility*, of what could happen. We find, for example, that '[t]he main structures of the global economic order must be designed to be fair to poor and developing countries' (Wilde 2011: 33). On one level that is a positive aim. If the global economic order was redesigned to advantage low- and middle-income nations then a great deal of suffering, poverty and poor health and wellbeing would be alleviated. For example, according to the World Health Organization (2020) life expectancy in 2019 for both sexes in nations such as Lesotho was 50.75, in Malawi 65.62 and in South Africa 65.25, which are all below the average global life expectancy of 73.2 years, and well below the average in high-income nations where average life expectancy for both sexes lies in the low 80s. The reasons for lower life expectancy and poorer all round wellbeing in low- and middle-income nations can be found in the complex ways that colonialism damaged all parts of colonized societies.

When the transitive verb 'have' is used that too is problematic. Consider another route that Nussbaum advocates: multinational corporations have responsibilities for promoting human capabilities in the regions in which they operate. The current model for doing so is corporate social responsibility (CSR). The basic tenet of CSR is that corporations (or any scale of business) can operate in a way that changes society, and the environment, for the better. Instead of just focusing on the economic bottom line, corporate entities can focus on a triple bottom line consisting of the three 'P's of people, profit and planet. On the surface, it is an appealing idea. Large global entities with considerable resources and influence re-engineer their operations to include projects that help people and nature. Take five seconds to read any large corporation's home pages and you see evidence of this move within business.

Some criticisms are easy to level against CSR. It is just an exercise in a multiplicity of woke-washing: green, rainbow, pink and so on. And that CSR can be exposed as a performativity of progressive action. While some CSR projects may yield some benefits for communities, workers or the environment, they are only projects within a larger context that still causes exploitation, damage and harm, whether to people or nature. A subtle critique of CSR is provided by Fleming et al (2013). They begin by drawing on Fisher (2009) and situating CSR as trapped with the horizons of capitalist realism. Good can only be achieved through the framework of capitalism: if you want to make the world a better place, then it can only happen if you have a multinational on board. But every multinational operates within the laws of capitalism. Profits are fundamental to their existence and that, at the end of the day, is all that counts. No corporation will sacrifice itself for an ethical goal.

The discussion so far identifies that Marx was indeed aware of wellbeing and that it played a central role in his understanding of the effects of alienation. What is needed now is a more fully worked-out model of wellbeing that places it in a more fully dialectical and materialist position that appreciates the various essential and internal relations that exist between the mind, body and society, which are absent in psychological and economic renderings of wellbeing. The answer is that there must be some form of dialectical relationship in play. Dialectics, after all, offers a mode of understanding that supposedly offers the possibility of holding and understanding complex relationships between opposite and contradictory objects.

So, what would a fuller account of a Marxist understanding of wellbeing be like and how could the various expression of alienation impair wellbeing? The next section tackles that question by speculating on how the four expressions of alienation could potentially impact on wellbeing. What ultimately emerges from the discussion here is a dialectical model of wellbeing that understands wellbeing as a state of being comprising many internal relations that exist between and within the embodied mindful human being and society. It points to how alienation gets under the skin and into the mind by translating social and historical phenomena into biological and psychological harm.

Towards an internally related dialectic of how alienation gets under the skin

I borrow part of the title for this section from social-epidemiologists Wilkinson and Pickett (2010, 2019). In the *Spirit Level* they begin to explore the relationships between how social agents experience inequality in their daily life and, in their words, how that translates into biological harms. They place emphasis on a variety of neuro-biological pathways that become activated in ways that are injurious to health and wellbeing. A considerable volume of work generated by biologist and neurologist Sapolsky (for a recent summary, see Sapolsky 2018) also emphasizes the connections of human biology and human society. Williams and Mohammed (2013), in their research on the relationships between race and health, also drew attention to the interactions of social processes and biological processes. They identify that racism at structural levels in the form of institutional or cultural racism is transmitted down what they term pathways of poor social resources in housing and class opportunities, which in turn lead to damaging psychological and physiological responses, leading to disability and poor physical and mental health.

Parallel to the work already mentioned, two developments in sociological theorization were under way: the sociology of the body and the sociology of emotions. In the late 1990s the embodied turn in sociology sought to reintroduce the body into sociology (see Schilling (2012) for greater detail). A vast literature was spawned at this time which sought to remedy an omission within sociology, that the discipline had lapsed into a form of idealism privileging the thoughts, interpretations and constructions of social agents. The body was for Schilling (2012) an 'absent presence'. It was missing in sociology. For medical sociology the turn to the body was necessary. As Simon Williams (2006) notes, the influence of post-modernism in the subdiscipline of medical sociology had restricted the body to the status of discourse. The privileging of Foucault and his meditations on power had drawn attention to how power is inscribed on bodies and how bodies are disciplined in different contexts, the recognition of a pre-discursive body, a fleshy sensuous body, had slipped away. The body was left, as Williams (2006: 6) noted, as 'disembodied, disembowelled, disincarnated or dematerialized'. He is talking about the visceral body, one with organs, one with a nervous system, and one that is vulnerable to disease and decline. Placing the body purely as a discursive entity narrows understanding of how poor health and wellbeing can emerge from social and economic relationships. How does a body that is purely discursive being disciplined in a certain way lead to a stroke or emotions such as depression if it is only a text? Pain, suffering, and all other major and minor discomforts and maladies can become visible. What returns is the awareness and importance of humans as fleshy, emotional entities where the presence of the biological reactions of the human body needs to be taken seriously.

Bringing the body back in does not mean a capitulation and return to biological readings of the body and engaging in a reductionist materialism. Warnings from Benton (1991) urge caution in doing so, and as Howson and Inglis (2001) too have warned, the discipline of biology is 'terra incognito' for sociologists, and sociologists risk moving into a field that is not their natural home and all the problems that may entail. A great many sociologists are squeamish and reticent to accept any role of biology in human society or in understanding a particular aspect of human existence, such as health. There are many good reasons why. Reference to biology can allow in crude forms of reductionism that humans are genetically predisposed to act in certain ways, that human genes are innately selfish, and therefore inequalities and hierarchies are natural and inescapable.

Brunner, though, has urged medial sociologists not to shy away from acknowledging the intervening processes at play between society and the human body:

> The senior sociologist Mildred Blaxter observed that researchers in the field of health inequalities find studying biology an awkward approach to explanation. While it is usual to measure social phenomena on the one hand and health on the other, the intervening processes tend to be avoided. There are at least two reasons for this avoidance: the danger of distraction from the social roots of health inequalities, and an antipathy to the 'biomedical model'. Sociology has tended to distance itself from the body. But we should not abstain, but recognise that social inequalities must generate biological inequalities. (Brunner 2009: 120)

One premise of alienation theory, as I have developed earlier, is that as well as humans possessing a human nature they are simultaneously natural, therefore biological, beings. If we are to accept a materialist position then we must accept the presence of the biological body. If we follow the philosophy of internal relations through it begins to indicate some distinct implications for wellbeing and the various relations between bodies, minds and society. The body, mind and society therefore cease to be three external objects that relate to each other as different molar entities but, instead, are infused in a myriad of multiple dialectical relations where the strict boundaries of each become much harder to sustain. It is not so much a simple triadic notion where the body emerges out of biology and society, but one where dialectical internal relations exist in society and in the body, as well as in and between the body and society. So, instead of thinking in terms of the binaries of body and society it is more fruitful to think in terms of various moments of embodiment and moments of society, which themselves are related to other bodily and social moments.

The philosophy of internal relations also requires an identification of the specific necessary relations involved in the historical transformation of what is under study. That is why I urge caution in uncritically using such undifferentiated terms such as the body and society, as it is specific relations and processes in each that are in relation with and between each other rather than the two entities themselves. There may be quite valid occasions when for the purposes of abstraction or exposition this is both a useful and a meaningful approach to take (as I do at points here) but for the purposes of analytical clarity it is necessary to bring out what in society relates to what in the biological.

The work of Marxist-inspired neuroscientist Rose (2006) assists in illustrating the inter-relationships of various dialectics, where distinct events in society flow with distinct biological processes. In describing how the brain works, Rose (2006: 62–65) draws our attention to an autopoietic understanding of the brain. He captures the brain as emerging from the internal relations of parts of the brain that rely on specificity (such as the motor cortex, where a set of neural connections develop that are not really shaped by external social experiences) and plasticity (variations and adaptations to the external environment or society). So rather than it being a straight 'race' between biology and environment, the two are inextricably linked: 'It is specificity and plasticity rather than nature and nurture that provide the dialectic within which development occurs, and both are utterly dependent on both genes and the environment' (Rose 2006: 64). Neuroscientist Damasio also draws attention to the internal relations of the body, and how the body, the mind, the brain, emotions and society are fundamentally enmeshed together and exist as a complex unity:

(1) The human brain and the rest of the body constitute an indissociable organism, integrated by means of mutually integrative biochemical and neural regulatory circuits (including endocrine, immune, and autonomic neural components); (2) The organism interacts with the environment as an ensemble: the interaction is neither of the body alone nor of the brain alone; (3) The physiological operations that we call mind are derived from structural and functional ensemble rather from the brain alone: mental phenomena can be fully understood only in the context of an organism's interacting in an environment. That environment is, in part, a product of the organism's activity itself and merely underscores the complexity of interactions we must take into account. (Damasio 2005: xvi–xvii)

The interplay of multiple moments and elements is similarly found in the work of Levins (2007; Levins and Lewontin 1985), who advances the metaphor of a triple helix of gene, organism and environment in his dialectical explanation of how biology and society animate each other. What Lewontin and Marxist biologist Levins also add to a dialectical understanding is an appreciation of history, and that the evolutionary process of humans exists in a historical context that unfolds across time, and where new challenges, whether created by humans or by nature, require new responses. This historical dimension is important to add to the discussion. What the work of Levins does, is to assist in avoiding one of the claims raised against Wilkinson in his inequality that he lapses into one of the sins of evolutionary psychology, where contemporary human beings are trapped with the evolutionary adaptations of their forebears in the Pleistocene era, between 2,588,000 and 11,700 years ago (Yuill 2010).

Other relations are also in effect that contribute to the dialectic being sketched out so far: the human mind is one, and the specific local and historical circumstances are others (relations that are themselves related to each other). The human biological body is not separate from the human conscious mind. As discussed earlier, following Damasio (2005), the human mind is not some idealist 'add on', or a spirit in the machine that for some unspecified reason came into being but the material outcome of evolutionary processes that came into existence as a response to demanding environmental conditions. The outcome of this was to allow *Homo sapiens* to develop certain capacities in order to survive. The capacities the human mind possesses involve the ability to reflect, to plan ahead, and to be aware of its existence and to be able to operate and act upon nature as opposed to merely reacting to it.

So, responses to conditions that are potentially alienating are not the same in every instance. These reactions can range from deciding on adaptive strategies (taking exercise to let off steam, for example), or to the countervailing strategies mentioned in Chapter 1 such as deciding on more oppositional or revolutionary strategies (joining a union or agitating for change in the workplace or in wider society). By drawing in the mind and the interpretative and reflective capacities of human beings it also addresses a weakness in the literature evident in the 1960s and 1970s empirical literature on alienation which focuses invariably on quantitative methods to measure and research alienation. How workers thought and how they reacted to and made sense of the conditions in which they worked is absent from those accounts.

Other influences may also pertain that affect how people experience negative conditions. As Eakin and MacEachen (1998) noted, poor wellbeing in the workplace depends on the local specifics of the workplace, where if greater unity, for instance, exists among the workforce then that can alter the experience and severity of the experiences of alienation. In that vein Muntaner et al (2002) have identified that countries where the level of trade union membership is higher exhibit all round better levels of health and wellbeing.

Wellbeing and the four expressions of alienation

If we accept that the human body and mind are in a series of internal dialectical relations with society and history then it opens fertile terrain to discuss the relationship between alienation and wellbeing, and how negative social events and relations translate into poor health and wellbeing. To do so, a variety of pieces of research are mobilized that even though they were never intended to explore the relationship between alienation and health could nevertheless illustrate and support the points that are made. The discussion is organized around the four expressions of alienation identifying the potential relations between social and biological processes.

Before proceeding further, the speculative nature of the forthcoming discussion on wellbeing and the four expressions of alienation requires a caveat. None of the research drawn on here was undertaken with any intention of engaging with alienation theory, and much of the various methodologies that were used would be questionable from a sociological perspective. For example, the psychological research drawn upon shares many of the weaknesses that one can level at most psychology: namely, that it operates at too restricted a level of abstraction, silent on deeper structural relations and tending to locate causality at an individual or near individual level (Parker 2007). However, that does not mean one can discard the results all together as they are indicative of how people operate in the workplace and trying to place them into a more structural anchorage can ameliorate those shortcomings, and they do point ahead to future research agendas and areas to explore. All I am saying here is that from the standpoint of alienation theory the various biological processes appear to be good candidates for how alienation as a social process relates to biological processes.

Process and product alienation

In the post-Marx alienation literature process alienation (the immediacy of engaging in the actual tasks of labour) appears as a frequent expression of alienation. Marx too in his writings also tended to focus on process alienation and in the research generated in the Whitehall II study it is, as Forbes and Wainwright (2001) have noted, issues of what could be categorized as process alienation that are to the fore in causing poor wellbeing. In this form of alienation issues of control and autonomy are paramount, where workers lack the opportunity to decide such aspects as how the work is organized and what latitudes they have in deciding how to structure their tasks. From a Marxian perspective the ability to exercise control and autonomy in work is a key element of human wellbeing. This form of alienation appears to negate the existence of – or at least impair – wellbeing.

Stress – as problematic as that term may be – is an obvious biological process to consider in a discussion of alienation and wellbeing. Some of Marx's descriptions of the problems facing workers appear to be similar to what would now be termed stress. Research into stress has revealed that it is a complex phenomenon, more than simply feeling pressured, and not just confined to the stereotype of the manager trying to balance a complex workload. Stress is much more likely to be found having negative consequences on workers rather than managers, and specifically those who lack control, autonomy and reward over their work (Marmot et al 1997, 1999).

Stress operates through the activation of the parasympathetic nervous system, in particular the 'fight-or-flight' response. This response is an evolutionary adaptation that allows not just humans but all mammals to respond to threat. It involves the temporary shutting down of physiological systems that are not essential for dealing with that threat and increasing the physiological systems that would be useful. The biochemical cortisol plays a critical role, acting as a messenger within the body signalling a change in state. So, functions such as cell repair and the immune system are suppressed in favour of systems that produce adrenalin and glucose, which in turn provide the body with increased energy in order for the threat to be either be evaded or combated. In the short term such a physiological state presents no problems, and can in some ways be beneficial to health, but when that state is activated on a long-term or constant basis then the problems begin. McEwan (2000) refers to this as allostatic load where the body is subject to a constant stream of stressors and begins to negatively adapt to noxious stimuli, resulting in a gradual wear-and-tear of the body, which, over time, can lead to serious health problems. The damaging physical and mental health consequences of chronic stress are widely researched and recorded, and include: depression, anxiety, stroke, fatigue, exhaustion, accelerated ageing, impaired cognitive function, increased abdominal fat and heart disease (Sapolsky 2004).

As Wainwright and Calnan (2002) warn, however, the stress discourse must be treated with caution: at worst it offers an understanding of a situation that is stripped of structural context, individualizes problems, renders workers as passive victims, and favours a linear causality as well as being guilty of biological reductionism. Referring back to how the embodied human agent exists within an ensemble of multiple relations provides one way out of reductionism.

Fellow human-being alienation

In this form of alienation people are either set against each other or lose contact with other human beings. Being social is a core aspect of Marxian anthropology, a core element of Marxist wellbeing, and an essential part of human species being, as it is cooperative labour that has played a critical role in allowing humans to be able to act on nature. If Marx is correct that being social is a natural genetic element of being human then one should be able to identify certain processes in the human body that allow for that to take place and perhaps play a role in health.

As the likes of Cacioppo and Cacioppo (2014) and Wilkinson and Pickett (2006) note, a raft of recent research has identified that being part of some form of social group is essential for positive health and wellbeing, and that this sociability is bound in with various biological processes that are activated when humans are in positive relations with each other. Part of the health-giving qualities of being social is related to the neuropeptide oxytocin, which, when active, produces the pleasant sensations and feelings humans experience when with others (Zak et al 2005, 2007; Carter 2017). As a biochemical, oxytocin plays an important role in influencing and coordinating various areas of the brain such as the amygdala and the hypothalamus and connecting those areas with the autonomic nervous system.

One important relation that oxytocin has with another part of the body is involved with the vagus nerve, which plays a role in keeping the heart beating at a regular and peaceful 72 beats per minute as opposed to 115 beats per minute, the pace at which the heart beats when we are stressed (Keltner 2009). While one could characterize cortisol (when it is over-produced as part of a stress reaction) as being a highly damaging biochemical in regards to health, then oxytocin is a useful biochemical in regards to health. Crucially the neuropeptide oxytocin only comes into play when in contact with other human beings. Not being in contact with other humans does not allow oxytocin to be expressed and therefore does not allow for the beneficial health state associated with oxytocin. So one can speculate that being alienated from other people does not allow for the release of this useful biochemical, which in turn means that its capacity to maintain health and wellbeing are affected.

The presence of oxytocin sounds highly positive. All that is required is to create situations where it is expressed, and we will love one another, solving many problems along the way. Summarizing research into oxytocin, Sapolsky (2018) urges caution, however, that oxytocin is not quite what some early research makes it out to be. The expression of oxytocin is dependent on *social* context. An interesting point given the dialectical relations of bodies, emotions, the social and so on that was developed earlier. It is active when humans are with a familiar in-group, with all the pleasant and beneficial effects that entails, but as De Dreu (2012; De Dreu and Kret 2016) established, oxytocin makes humans less loving and caring – if not hostile – to an out-group. The research is silent on how group identities form, not surprising as that is not the researchers' domain, but there is plenty of sociology that attests to how people form in-groups based on workplace identities, national identities (B. Anderson 2016) and the whole arc of Elias' (2000) work on how ever more social humans have become. I feel this point adds to what I say about alienation, if we are in relations of solidarity with others then health and wellbeing benefits can follow, alienated and fragmented from others then the opposite can happen. The reasons for the existence of solidarity and alienation remain resolutely in the social.

Human–nature alienation

This expression of alienation refers to the deeper moments of alienation where the human agent is denied the ability to exercise their creativity and to use their abilities in a way that allows for self-realization and for the betterment of other fellow humans. How this form of alienation may be translated into poor health may understood by drawing on some recent work from psychology on flow (when someone is completely immersed in and absorbed by a task) and on boredom (when someone is engaged in tasks that are stifling and deadening).

The psychology of flow broadly states that human beings enter a state of full awareness, immersion and concentration when engaged in a task (Csikszentmihalyi 1990, 1997; Seligman 2002; Liu and Csikszentmihalyi 2020). Being engaged in a flow experience allows for at least some momentary self-realization where all one's capacities are actively engaged in the creative execution and pursuit of an activity. Often this involves going beyond what one is comfortable with and engaging in something that is creative and challenging. The descriptions of flow as advanced by Csikszentmihalyi are akin to Marx when he refers in the *Economic and Philosophic Manuscripts* to humans achieving a historical period where self-actualization occurs and people are free to engage in non-alienating activity.

There also appears to be a wellbeing benefit to being immersed in the flow of an activity. Research has associated those who report flow experiences with positive outcomes such as greater overall life satisfaction, less stress, and a general all round perception of being happy. Unfortunately, flow experiences seem to be rare in society. Csikszentmihalyi (1990) found that 40 per cent of participants in a survey have never enjoyed a flow experience. From the standpoint of alienation theory this should not be surprising as the structures of society act against people expressing their creativity. So, what about the reverse, when there is no flow, when there is a deadening stasis or boredom prevails? The psychology of boredom reveals one outcome of boredom: that it is possible to be 'bored to death' and that boredom, at least in its chronic form, can have serious deleterious effects on health and wellbeing.

Summarizing the research on boredom and health, Eastwood et al (2012: 482) note that boredom is associated with depression and anxiety, alexithymia, somatization complaints, alcohol misuse, over-eating, and can be problematic for people with schizophrenia and other chronic mental health issues. There are, of course, also basic health and safety issues where boredom can lead to a lack of attention and accidents. More interesting is the body of work that focuses explicitly on the relation of chronic boredom with sense of meaning and purpose in life. What this research indicates is that for people who encounter and experience chronic boredom on a regular, if not daily, level, then it leads to a deeper sense of malaise and a negation of self.

As discussed earlier, Fanon (2021b) wrote extensively about the damage of alienation created by colonialism where colonized people have their history, identities, culture and self erased by the violence of colonial rule. These writings also provide insights into how alienation affects human nature and wellbeing. The historical effects of which are still evident today. The work of Williams and Mohammed's (2013) mentioned above in South Africa indicates that the historical hierarchical of race during the Apartheid period exerts a strong influence on the health of racialized groups today. The Apartheid system constructed different ethnic categories – Blacks, Whites, Indians and Coloured – the purpose of which was brutal violent separation of people and the negation of control over their live. This situation can be read through Fanon as a form of human nature alienation, where social agents are denied their own history and culture.

Conclusion

In this chapter I moved to drawing linkages between alienation and wellbeing. If anything, alienation is about poor wellbeing, it is about suffering, it is about social agents' lives being abbreviated, shortened and made less than they both could be or, normatively, *should* be. Alienation's effect on wellbeing operates on different levels. It can be resorting to opioids when all the stable reference points, symbolic resources on which identity are built, are consumed by the anarchic fluctuations of capital and the pursuit of profit. It can also a daily exposure of harm in following instructions, and lacking freedom to exercise creativity or input into the labour process. Chapter 4 provides a case study of alienation and its effects on one group of workers.

4

Case Study: Social Workers,
the Compassionate Self and
Disappointed Jugglers

Frances's story

"They got lost," said Frances. She was an experienced social worker with years of service behind her. The profession had changed quite a bit in that time. She could recall a time when her day-to-day work was with people, discussing their problems, why they had become a client, as they used to say, of social work services and how they could work together to overcome the challenges that they faced. When they did find a way forward, solutions to the problems that the client faced, that gave her a buzz, a feeling of really achieving something. That is why she had decided to become a social worker: to make a difference to people's lives. She liked her job, she liked her colleagues and she liked the clients with whom she worked.

Over the last 20 years social work had changed considerably. The changes were always small, a drip-feed of new protocols, subtle changes in management, and an increasing emphasis on recording the progress of each client, though they were now called service-users. All of those little changes eventually added up. The job was now totally different. The team in her office began to work longer and longer hours. Lunchtime disappeared. There was just so much to do and the pressure to complete tasks and meet benchmarks was unyielding. Anyone who took any time off from their work to grab a five-minute coffee or, heaven forbid, leave the office to buy a sandwich was immediately treated with suspicion: why could they take time away from their desk? They mustn't have enough to do. The easy and happy camaraderie between colleagues disappeared.

The ever-increasing workload was bad enough, but what really frustrated her most, made her depressed, angry and frustrated, was that she hardly ever saw a client. That was always the highlight of the day, meeting someone and sitting down and trying to work things through with them. Instead, it was report after report after report. Endless reports to fill in that had obviously not been designed by a social worker. The reports somehow imagined that clients' lives improved in nice straight lines that could be measured on some arbitrary scale. Nonsense, for every step forward, there were three steps backward or two sideways. Real people with real problems do not behave in that way. Their lives were complex and messy.

That's what she meant when she said "They got lost," real people with real problems became lost from her and lost in the paperwork.

Introduction

In this chapter I wish to bring together the points I have been raising in the previous chapters in an empirical case study. The study of alienation can never be simply a philosophical exercise. All theories, especially in the Marxist tradition, require to be tested in the empirical flow of history. Doing so is vital to keep a theory alive, relevant and to allow it to develop. Unless dialogue exists between theory and empirical research, then the study of alienation will be a dead project. Marxist methodology differs from other methodologies in that it draws more on German traditions of *Wissenschaft*, which unlike British traditions of empiricism is more concerned with developing a line of reasoning and argument rather than positing absolute proof. That tradition is most evident in the role that theory undertakes in Marx's research. When a theory is used in research it is not deployed with the intention of proving or refuting it but with the intention of further refining and developing that theory. That presence of continual refinement as part of the Marxist research programme has led several Marxist commentators, such as Callinicos (1982) and Little (2011), to liken Marx's approach to that of Lakatos (1980), whose understanding of science claimed that the hard core of a research programme comprises of certain theories and concepts that are fundamental to that programme and that auxiliary hypotheses are generated in order to add explanatory power to the overall programme:

> The negative heuristic of the programme forbids us to direct the modus tollens at this 'hard core'. Instead, we must use our ingenuity to articulate or even invent 'auxiliary hypotheses', which form a protective belt around the core, and we must redirect the modus tollens to these. It is the protective belt of auxiliary hypotheses which has to bear the brunt of tests and get adjusted and re-adjusted, or even completely replaced, to defend the thus-hardened core. A research programme is successful if all this leads to a progressive problemshift; unsuccessful if it leads to a degenerating problemshift. (Lakatos 1980: 48)

Research can therefore add to a theory not by directly supporting it, but instead by developing new additions to the theory that bolt onto the original theory, thereby refining and improving on its core assumptions. Marxist Burawoy (1998) calls on Lakatos in his extended case study technique for this very reason. As he says, 'we seek reconstructions that leave core postulates intact, that do as well as the preexisting theory upon which they are built, and that absorb anomalies with parsimony, offering novel angles of vision' (Burawoy 1998: 16).

At its simplest Marx's methodology involves deconstructing what he regards as a very complex, dynamic and internally related world into smaller, more manageable units of inspection, before reintegrating those smaller pieces after analysis back into the whole again. This three-part strategy is most associated with Marx's discussion of method outlined in the 1857 *Preface*, which many regard as the clearest example of Marx outlining his methodology (see Hall 2003). It is here that he runs through and outlines that three-part method where reality is accessed by beginning with the concrete and actual world, of how things really are as we encounter them in daily life, before theorizing that empirical observation in order to unlock the many determinations of which it comprises, before finally returning to the empirical and concrete world again but this time with a much richer and deeper understanding of that world. The usual convention is to symbolize this method is as follows:

$$A - B - A1$$

'A' here represents the real concrete world, 'B' the movement to theorize that observation highlighting its complexities and determinations, and 'A1' the return to the concrete world, but one that has been made much more understandable and richer by bringing to the surface all its many parts. There are obvious parallels here with Hegel in that his dialectic returns us to the point of departure but at a much higher level of knowledge and understanding. Indeed, in *Capital* Marx comments on how much comfort and inspiration he drew from Hegel. This proximity with Hegel has to, however, be treated with caution. Marx is very clear in *The Critique* that while he may cut close to a Hegelian wind he ultimately steers a very different course. The main point of separation is that for Hegel it is only the thinking mind that matters, while for Marx the thinking mind is important but the real concrete world is unaltered by that mental activity existing independently of thought. It is this emphasis on the material that marks for Della Volpe (1980) and Zelený (1980) the scientific nature of Marx's methodology, where instead of projecting a priori philosophy onto the world as Hegel had done and hypostatizing the speculative into the real, Marx begins with the concrete and creates his understanding from that basis.

There are two important elements in Marx's methodology that are useful to highlight in relation to how he understands the concrete world that forms the 'A' as discussed earlier. The first is that Marx (1991: 956) understood that there was more to society than simply what occurs on the surface everyday empirical level, as captured in the following lines from *Capital III*: 'all science would be superfluous if the outward appearance and the essence of things directly coincided'. As Zelený (1980) emphasizes, Marx sets himself the task in his work to uncover the core relations and logical forms of capitalism, and to journey into the fundamental relations of capitalism in order to understand how it both produces and reproduces itself through time and history.

One technique that can assist in that process of returning data into a dialectical context is to begin with a process of what Eco (1983) terms 'overcoded abduction', involving the redescription or recontextualization of data into a theoretical framework. Meyer and Lunnay (2012) advocate its use within theory-driven research, while Habermas (1978) commends abduction for its ability to create new knowledge. Abduction is a particular form of inference that Magnani defines as follows: 'Abduction is the process of inferring certain facts and/or laws and hypotheses that render some sentences plausible, that explain or discover some (eventually new) phenomenon or observation; it is the process of reasoning in which explanatory hypotheses are formed and evaluated' (Magnani 2007: 273).

Abduction therefore develops new knowledge – synthetic knowledge in the Kantian sense – by providing fresh insights through the recontextualization or redescription of social phenomena. This requires placing an existing known event or experience into a different conceptual framework. Aspects of what existed before are now seen in a new light that crystallizes and abstracts important elements and moments of those phenomena leading to new discoveries. Induction and deduction conversely begin and end with a reassembling of what is already known or experienced at the empirical level – analytic knowledge in the Kantian sense – and thus are incapable of developing the same novelty of which abduction is capable. As Peirce (1992: 198), the originator of abduction as a form of logical inference, notes, abductive 'reasoning infers very frequently to a fact not capable of direct observation'. One indicative example of abduction is Darwin's recontextualization of human development as evolution (Jensen 1995). By doing so Darwin opened up new insights into humanity. One of these was that if humans evolved from primates then human ancestry had to begin in Africa, as he claimed in *The Descent of Man*. This prediction was an inference only made possible from a process of abduction, as Darwin was working purely through the limited empirical knowledge of the time and within his theory of evolution without the benefits and advantages of modern DNA analysis or archaeology that have now empirically vindicated the contention he made a hundred years ago.

As a form of inference abduction does not necessarily follow the accepted laws of logic as can be found in deduction and induction. Instead, it operates in a variety of ways which exhibit the commonality of reasoning and making arguments where the best possible case is made given how one moves between a piece of data (result) and a theory (law). Abduction's main use in social science research is to assist in identifying relations between empirical events and either theoretical perspectives or normative social codes. Danermark et al identify how abduction can be used in social scientific research thus:

(1) have an empirical event/ phenomenon (the result), which we (2) relate to a rule, which (3) leads us to a new supposition about the event/ phenomenon. But in social science research the rule is often a frame of interpretation or a theory, and the conclusion (the case) is a new interpretation of a concrete phenomenon – an interpretation that is plausible given that we presuppose that the frame of interpretation is plausible. (Danermark et al 2002: 90)

What is achieved at the end of this process is not an iron-cast result but some form of hypothesis, albeit one that is highly supported by a reasoned argument based on the data that has been presented.

One clear example of where Marx uses some form of abduction can be found in *Capital* in the section on the factory. As part of *Capital*, it is a unique section in that it is the only part of *Capital* where Marx actually discusses in any depth actual capital and real historical events, about what was happening around him in the early phases of industrialization. Here we find a mass of empirical evidence both observational and statistical that is conveyed from the perspective of his philosophical anthropology, with, as identified earlier in the literature review, many passages reading like passages from the *Manuscripts*. What he achieves by doing so is to demonstrate how these are indicative of his theories of human labour and alienation.

Abduction also provides another important function guarding against some potential pitfalls associated with theory-driven research such as that being undertaken here. Meyer and Lunnay summarize one potential danger of the theory so dominating the research that material and data that does not quite fit becomes ignored:

We argue that abductive inference is fundamental to theory-driven research. The defining characteristic of theory-driven research, that it uses theory a priori (Montgomery et al. 1989), forms the basis of its perceived weaknesses. A central critique is that given the structured nature of the research, the researcher cannot logically identify the unintended artefacts of empirical data – the experiences of the participants are filtered through the theoretical lens (Coryn et al. 2010). The use of abductive inference enables researchers to address this critique by moving the analysis beyond the theoretical frame. (Meyer and Lunnay 2012: 2.7)

This refers back to the earlier point made concerning the Lakatosian nature of Marxian research, in that it is not a simple case of refutation or proof, but rather a process whereby the hard core of the theory is enriched by further developing that hard core with the addition of auxiliary hypotheses. Meyer and Lunnay point out also that abduction assists in widening out the overall return of the effort expended in the research by not only allowing for theoretical refinement but also the capture of empirical material:

> Additionally, theory-driven researchers have been accused of conducting empirical research for the sole purpose of testing theory, rather than the empirical outcomes (Stufflebeam and Shinkfield 2007). The application of abductive inference assists the researcher to overcome this potential bias and to give theory-driven research greater transparency. The iterative process of analysis using this form of inference expands the initial theoretical assumptions and extends the research beyond a deductive analysis. The researcher further investigates the traditionally unexplored findings throughout data collection and analysis, revealing a more comprehensive understanding of the theoretical frame, while pursuing quality empirical outputs. (Meyer and Lunnay 2012: 2.7)

In this case study an abductive approach was used in the analysis of the data. A fuller account of the adductive method can be found elsewhere (Yuill 2017). I followed the steps outlined earlier by first generating data through interviews using fairly conventional semi-structured interview techniques. Once the data had been coded, using a deviant case approach, I then related those codes to the frame of interpretation (alienation theory) in order to establish either new insights into alienation theory or to further support that alienation theory can make sense of complex social phenomena.

The case study

Social workers were selected on the grounds that they provide a counterintuitive group of workers to research. Previous research on alienation focuses almost exclusively on manual or factory workers of various skills with scant attention on how professional workers are affected by capitalism. The need to focus across different forms of workers is an important point to pick up as Marx conjectured that all forms of workers regardless of their place in the means of production will one day be subsumed into abstract labour. The process of being subsumed into abstract labour is occurring within social work with various managerial tactics and logics being imported from the private sector into the public sector over the last three decades, resulting in what Carey (2008) has deemed a radical reform of the sector. That reform has resulted in a deprofessionalization of social work alongside reductions in autonomy and an intensification of work. The dynamic of reducing all forms of labour into abstract labour is almost poetically captured in the *Communist Manifesto*: 'The bourgeoisie has stripped of its halo every occupation hitherto honoured and looked up to with reverent awe. It has converted the physician, the lawyer, the priest, the poet, the man of science, into its paid wage labourers' (Marx 1998: 5).

A brief history of British social work from parochial professionalism to audit culture

Reading through the extensive literature on social work a narrative emerges of a profession that has been subject to a number of regressive reforms that have considerably transformed social work from how it was in the pre-neoliberal days of the 1960s and 1970s. The profession then operated with greater autonomy as part of the welfare state in a period that Harris (1998) refers to as 'parochial professionalism'. Evans (2010: 52) defines parochial professionalism as being centred around loyalty to the immediate fieldwork team, the capacity to exercise considerable discretion and autonomy in judgements concerning service-users, and a distinctive and equal relationship with managers. What management that did exist exercised its authority not on the grounds of hierarchical location but rather by appeals to the individual manager's skills as a practitioner (Harris 1998). Individual social workers could practice and exercise greater levels of discretion and autonomy with no real accountability or recourse to anyone else let alone management as would be currently understood (see Parsloe and Stevenson 1978).

No discussion of social work and the changes it has undergone since the late 1970s is complete without mention of the Radical Social Work Movement (RSWM), which existed roughly from the early to late 1970s. The RSWM was not strictly a movement but more a coalition of social workers who shared some form of disenchantment with how social work services were provided and how the situation of client groups could be improved in a capitalist society. Alongside Marxist perspectives on welfare, feminist, Black liberation and gay activist perspectives informed a position on how both the welfare state and the state generally could be altered in order to meet the needs of minority or excluded groups, if not lead to a wholesale transformation of society that would dismantle the various structural roots of oppression and exclusion.

Critically there was no 'Orgreave moment' for social work, as befell sections of workers such as British miners in the 1980s, when the massed ranks of social work came into contact with the full force of the state. Rather the road to social work becoming a quasi-business was paved with a series of small-step policy interventions: changes in workplace culture by importing and imposing business discourses; the introduction of managerialism; the reframing of service-users as consumers; and government regulation of social work education. It is not implied here that by describing the changes that have been imposed on social work over the last three or so decades as consisting of small steps that these are not significant in terms of their effects or the consequences they had on the lifeworlds of individual social workers. Rather, social work was not subject to the same neoliberal overt frontal assault that other sections of workers experienced in the 1970s and 1980s, such as the aforementioned miners in Britain (Milne 2014) or in other countries experiencing the neoliberal revolution such as public sector workers in New York (Freeman 2001).

The parochial professionalism and the political radicalism of the RSWM came under strain from the 1980s onwards as a result of both Conservative and Labour governments implementing various reforms that sought to fundamentally alter the basic structures of the British state. Each government made those reforms in their different ways mediated by the historical origins of their political ideologies. The Third Way (Giddens 1998) policies of the Labour Party sought to provide a social democratic gloss to the implementation of further marketization and privatization with rhetoric concerning equality and fairness. The first step change for social work was the increasing presence of management and a managerialist culture within social work and with it the introduction of a constant feature of much of the critical commentary on contemporary social work: paperwork. The discussion earlier touched upon how the neoliberal state leads to the appearance of a new form of management that sought to reorder social work.

What occurred throughout the 1980s and 1990s was a familiar process of devaluing professionalism: the dominance of the manager and managerial knowledge over professional knowledge, financial imperatives trumping care and concern, and the market being the environment in which work occurs (Tsui and Cheung 2004). A parallel reordering of the work that social workers performed in their daily working lives also occurred. The new managerialism brought with it a requirement to evaluate and monitor what happens in the workplace resulting in an increased emphasis on record-keeping and paperwork in order to assess performance. These again are mechanisms by which greater control can be exerted by the new management as they lay out for inspection what a worker does in a day.

As Dardot and Laval state, the neoliberal impulse to evaluate does allow for greater managerial control but also goes much deeper in attempting to transform what it is to be a professional within the public sector:

> Measuring performance has become the elementary technology of power relations in public services. … It tends to shape the activity itself and aims to produce subjective changes in the 'evaluated', so they meet their 'contractual commitments' to higher bodies. This

involves reducing the autonomy acquired by a number of professional groups, such as doctors, judges and teachers, who are deemed to be expensive, lax or unproductive, by imposing on them the criterion of results constructed by a proliferating expert technostructure. (Dardot and Laval 2013: 250)

One can easily add social workers to this list, but the points they make concerning subjective changes and reductions in autonomy are relevant here as can be seen when we consider how cultures of evaluation and paperwork have been introduced into social work. As Munro (2004) notes in her analysis of the rise of paperwork and an audit culture within social work the profession moves from a highly relaxed culture in terms of recording activities, in line with Harris' parochial professionalism, to one where the daily routine of social work is defined by the disciplinary technologies of audit trails and bureaucratic obligations. While not denying that a certain level of paperwork and recording of what occurs in the field is necessary, it is the extent, scope and the reach of the paperwork that is the problem. Her verdict on the effects of this trend towards greater auditing of the actions of social workers is negative.

Neoliberalist policies of both Labour and Conservative governments have exerted a considerable impact on the profession of social work, changing it almost beyond recognition from how it was once practised in the United Kingdom (Jones 2001; Ferguson 2008). As social work is tied into the state, whether on a local or national scale, it more than other professions has been and remains particularly sensitive to changes in the purpose and remit of the state (Lymbery 2012). Social work as a profession has occupied a contested and contradictory space within society and within the overall means of production (Corrigan and Leonard 1978). Traditionally, social workers have regarded themselves as being engaged in some form of progressive role, attempting to create some form of equity and protection for vulnerable and neglected members of society that have been left behind due to social location or social identity, whether that is by class, gender, ethnicity, sexuality or disability, and so on. However, in addition to that progressive role, social work has also operated to some extent on behalf of the state, regulating and controlling those on the margins of society who may be understood as being problematic for the smooth operation of capitalist accumulation. In effect, social work could be seen to be a non-uniformed wing of state control and an integral element of state governance.

Working within an avowedly Marxist framework, and writing in the dying days of British Labourism, Corrigan and Leonard (1978) attempted to tease out that contradiction without defaulting to either element of that contradiction. They posit a sophisticated and nuanced approach to understanding the relationship of the social worker with the welfare state.

They are critical of simplistic notions of the welfare state that its existence only seeks to serve the interests of the ruling class and is therefore an oppressive force within society, and also of uncritically accepting social workers as frontline revolutionaries in the battle for a fairer society:

> This analysis of the State in general and the welfare state in particular, has emphasised its contradictory nature and the necessity of understanding these contradictions. Social work operates at one of the most significant interfaces of those contradictions. Social workers, as state employee, often enhance and negate human welfare within the same processes of their work, and it is by understanding these processes that the possibility of more radical practice exists. (Corrigan and Leonard 1978: 106)

In the 1960s public services provided by the state were perceived as being rightfully outside the sphere of the private sector and the only place where services such as social work could be located as they would provide the most equitable mechanism for the provision of social care (Marshall 1981). That was before the historical appearance of the New Right and neoliberalism from the late 1970s onwards that instituted a new and radical conception of the state, its relationship with citizens and what the fundamental purpose of the state is about.

It is useful to clarify the object within a Marxist framework that social workers produce before proceeding further. Their object of production is, after all, the positive transformation of a vulnerable and marginalized human being, at an individual, familial or community level. The noun 'object' by itself may strike a utilitarian or instrumental note since it is people who are being referred to in the case of social work, but for Marx the objects of human production are imbued with the consciousness of the maker and stand for much more than a simple thing or presence. Lefebvre captures how the object in Marxian thought exceeds mundane definitions:

> For child and adult alike, objects are not merely a momentary material presence, or the occasion of a subjective activity; they provide us with an objective social content. Traditions (technical, social, spiritual) and the most complex qualities are present in the humblest of objects, conferring on them a symbolic value or 'style'. Each object is a content of consciousness, a moment. (Lefebvre 1968: 128)

Results and analysis
The compassionate self and the choice of social work as a profession
One of the first questions that the interview sought to elicit were the reasons why the participants had chosen social work as a profession. As

the subsequent coding indicated, a 'compassionate self' emerged from the interviews. The core of this compassionate self was a concern for the welfare for others and an 'other-directedness' where the positive enhancement of the situation of people experiencing some form of distress or disadvantage was crucial to self-identity. For the majority of participants in the interviews, the compassionate self was a life-long commitment to other people that emerged out of childhood experiences of either being from a family which worked in the care sector (not just social work but also professions such as nursing), or from witnessing a close friend or other family member not receiving the support they required during a time of distress or hardship. That experience in turn prompted and influenced their choice of career later in life, by selecting an occupation that provided the opportunity to offer the help that they thought was missing and should be there, or to carry on a family tradition of being involved in one of the many caring public services. Such an experience had become core to their subjectivities and sense of self, as the following extracts typify:

'I think that it was experiences that I had had when I was younger. I had seen a lot of people in need and there wasn't any response to that and I felt that I wanted to be with that person. To fill in that contradiction.' (Jennifer)

'Yeah, all through school I wanted to do a job meeting people and working with people and helping people. My mum was very much focused on that area as well. ... I didn't want to be stuck in front of a computer all the time, superficial contact, the more in-depth not working in that kind of area you know, but in-depth touch with people.' (Rachel)

'I suppose my mum, she had a social "workie" background. She wasn't a social worker as such, but she was sort of helping people with learning difficulties, residential care home settings. ... Just seemed like an obvious choice really.' (Kate)

That personal narrative was also strongly voiced by Rebecca, who recounts her very personal experiences of family separation where a social worker, from her perspective at the time, failed to identify and act on the subtleties of her situation. This combination of both experiencing personal distress in her own biography coupled with her perception of the shortcomings of a particular social worker had prompted her from the early age of 12 into wanting to become a social worker in adulthood:

'I didn't think that the social worker really picked up on any of the things that I was saying so it kind of frustrated me a wee bit, you know, that this woman has come and asked me questions but not really seeing what I'm trying to tell her. So I suppose from that moment onwards I kinda knew from the age of 12 that I kinda wanted to be a social worker so that I'd be understanding of what children you know the kinda situation like that again I'd kinda want to make sure that I wouldn't do what that social worker done.' (Rebecca)

Those that did not indicate a personal experience or familial tradition of working in care indicated that the main impulse for them was not to work in an office but instead to engage in some form of meaningful work with people:

'I wanted to work with people, like I say, get away from computers. … It's probably because just that I have a caring sort of nature, and I just like relating to people, working with people. Like I enjoy time with clients, hearing about their issues and helping them find ways of resolving their issues. … I suppose it's something in my nature maybe.' (Sheila)

The urge to work in an environment free of computers recurred throughout Sheila's interview. Sarah and Fiona, who both wished to work in a profession that offered some form of meaning, also shared that dislike of office work voiced by Sheila. Fiona noted that she wanted to get away from "computers, nine-to-five, not having a sense of function or purpose as such". Craig, meanwhile, described how he sought a job that offered the opportunity to help and work with people that contrasted with the industrial work into which other males in his family had entered.

Richard, who had come into social work later in life, did not record some form of personal experience or familial tradition of caring for others. In his case, it was his socialist beliefs that provided his motive for becoming a social worker. Those socialist beliefs for him implied a set of guiding ethical norms that being other-directed and working for the benefit of others was a positive, socially useful and intrinsically morally good path to follow, as the following quote indicates: "Like I said if you dig deeper, I'm quite socialist in ideology and I just ken that there should be a state-provided back up. You know, I think societies are judged by how well they look after the people who are least able to function in society." What we therefore find is that becoming a social worker was motivated by a core aspect of self. That core being formed here by childhood experiences, family traditions, political beliefs or the wish to engage in activity that held some form of meaning. The desired object of labour is the positive improvement in the life and wellbeing of another social being. It is that core aspect which forms what becomes alienated in the labour process, the impulse to make positive change and to find meaning in labour.

Why the participants decided to become social workers strongly shaped their relation with the product of their work and this provenance exerts an influence on their subsequent experiences of alienation. In the personal narratives of the participants a strong desire and motivation to help and improve the lives of other people was highly evident, which fits into the 'Compassionate Self' category. The desire to help was therefore a core part of the participants' ideas of who they are: an essential element of their self and identity, acting as an animating motivation both behind their career choices and in their personal lives, becoming a central feature of their consciousness, their way of being in the world. It was not just in the opening phase of the interview when the interviewees were directly asked why they wanted to become social workers, but an orientation that was visible and evident throughout the interviews.

The compassionate self requires to be abducted into Marxist alienation theory. It can be in three ways. (1) The participants' talk of a deeper caring self and the desire for labour to be meaningful is congruent with Marxian anthropology and theory of human nature, where the quality and purpose of work is important in terms of, recalling Wood, reaching some form of self-actualization where the rewards of labour are more than financial. A further connection with Marxian anthropology can be made (2) in that the participants wish for their work to involve the intersubjective transformation of social agents – it is therefore other directed and social, a critical part of how Marx understands humans to be. The compassionate self, finally, also (3) provides what it is, in this particular instance, from which a worker is estranged and alienated. How the compassionate self fares in the hidden abode of work is tackled next.

The disappointed juggler and the realities of social work

The social workers expected that they would be able to exercise their compassionate self in their work, and for their labour to act as a medium for the realization of their compassionate self. In reality that opportunity to exercise their core beliefs and construct of self did not happen to the extent for which they had wished. The 'disappointed juggler' theme emerged from the interviews, taking its name from the reference to work being akin to a juggler having to keep an eye on many different functions without letting any of them drop.

Throughout the interviews the overwhelming presence of report writing was noted by all of the participants (the "nature of the beast", as Kate said) and that the report writing dominated all other concerns to the point of reducing available time that could be spent working with service-users.

'I used to think when I first left university that most of my time would be spent with clients. But in actual fact most of your time is spent doing the paperwork and doing case notes. So, you maybe get a third of your working week actually with people and the other two-thirds taken up just by purely with paperwork.' (Sarah)

'[T]his paperwork is too much, it's ridiculous. … You don't stop. This is crazy, this is ridiculous. Look at all these forms, look at the length of all these forms, they're repetitive. Some of this care plan is irrelevant to what we provide now, eligibility criteria for example. For me it doesn't really change things for the better as far as I can see.' (Kate)

'Paperwork and stuff? It's disproportionate! I was trying to work it out the other day. It's probably about, with the adult protection thing, it's increased a bit. Probably of the five days a week, probably, there is some assessment clinics like meetings to go to. Probably only two days a week I'm seeing folk out the five.' (Richard)

A feeling of frustration at the extent of paperwork and how all other aspects of work were subordinated to it was palpable:

'When I first went into social work here is the stuff that you want to actually do with the families and you do not get so much of an opportunity to do that.' (Rachel)

'It's not what I signed up for. We obviously do assessments, I think a lot of the time the assessments we've identified what we need but there's not always access to what we say we need.' (Jennifer)

'I thought it was going to be more about contact with clients, you know, motivating change in people's lives, rather than being on a desk writing out reports that are due in a certain time/timeframe.' (Peter)

The importance of actively and consciously producing some form of object in the external world is an essential tenet of Marxian philosophical anthropology and where the influence of Hegel is most keenly felt. So, the question then arises: what was the product, the object of labour on which the participants laboured (or, as we shall see, were supposed to labour)? It was either the damaged lives of people living on the margins of society, people with long-term health issues and disabilities, or those who had in some way violated social norms. To that extent the interviewees were not working with the classic objects of material labour (making cars or working in factories) but instead were working with the new forms of immaterial labour as described by Hochschild (1983) and Sayers (2007, 2013): the emotional states of other human beings. Thus, the objectification of creative labour for the social workers was some form of change in the lives of the service-users with whom they worked where the service-user would be better placed to cope with the problems that were presenting in their lives. The labour power required of the social workers takes the form of the exercise of emotional resources such as empathy, alongside the practice of a number of learned skills such as cognitive behavioural therapy and other similar techniques.

In practice the historical form of alienation in this case study was the object of labour. Instead of the object of labour taking the embodied form of effecting change in the life of a service-user, the object of labour the social workers desired, it was instead the mind-numbing and alienating completion of paperwork, in particular the case report. The case report is meant to document the situation of the service-user, identifying their needs and so forth, working in parallel with the actual casework performed by the social worker. From what the participants indicated in their interviews the report in effect replaced the service-user to whom it referred and became the object of work, the completion of the paperwork taking precedence over the actual person on who it was based, becoming an end in itself as opposed to a means to an end:

'I had a false image in my head of what social work would be about, there would be tons of resources available, to just be able to throw at people who needed them or wanted them. The reality was quite different. Having to go in front of panels to request things. It's just not a case of doing an assessment and requesting funding, you've also got to then justify it to a panel of people because funding's so tight just now. That is the situation the whole country is in and maybe jump through hoops sounds a bit kinda em performing for your payment. There are a lot of steps to go through I suppose I didn't even consider beforehand.' (Joe)

Probably one of the more telling remarks about the dominance of paperwork and bureaucracy and how it shaped their working lives was Frances' reply when asked about the clients or service-users in her daily work, as she had not mentioned them that much in the interview, referring in the main to paperwork and tight budgets: "They got lost," she replied.

A report should not be mistaken for a neutral bureaucratic task. It needs to be understood as the distillation of various power relations that shape both the lifeworld of the service-user and the social worker. As Fahlgren (2009) and Munro (2004, 2011) point out, the report is constructed by forces external to professional social workers. They have little say in the context, format and structure of the report. Instead, it is government agencies that create a document that is in line with dominant ideologies and political responses to moral panics elsewhere in society. Under current neoliberalism the report institutionalizes the accelerated improvement of a service-user in a linear temporal trajectory that does not allow for the complexity of service-users' needs and lives (Pösö and Eronen 2015). The report with its armoury of Likert scales and milestones also serves as a disciplinary restraint on the social worker. Their autonomy and decision-making latitude is reduced to a narrow instrumental horizon.

The report, not the service-user, therefore, becomes the de facto object of labour: the product of what they do. So, the removal of the product here is not achieved by the product leaving the factory gates containing all the workers' expended labour power (the input of mental and physical skills, talents and abilities) but rather by a substitution of the desired object of labour, the one that would lead to them realizing the reasons why they wanted to be social workers, with one that negates and denies that desire.

If we note what the participants said about the impact that report writing had on their time, their wellbeing and how it occupied the temporal horizon of the workplace and their consciousness, it matches Marx's description of the effects of product and process alienation in the *Manuscripts*. He describes there how the product becomes more important than the worker: a reified entity looming over the worker, negatively absorbing their energies (whether physical or mental or both) and not replenishing them with anything in return. Many of the interviewees reported that they could never get on top of their paperwork, feeling that it could never be tamed or controlled, and that it was the cause of many of their problems with work.

'I find it stressful and demanding and exhausting. I came in with a real positive outlook but now: it is very negative.' (Frances)

'I think there are a lot of people who don't verbalise how busy they are, how stressed they feel. They do go unchecked and unnoticed and you sometimes find their ... caseloads, you know, increasing the level of their bitterness, increasingly you notice that they can't lift their head from their desk even for five minutes. They get sort of physically unwell and they sort of fatigue.' (Peter)

'Sometimes you are aware of being pressured at other times not ... but I think you have to be robust physically and emotional within yourself just to do this job. ... I had three/four months off and felt I was ready to come back to work, but when I did you realise very quickly that you can still be quite fragile.' (Nathan)

One deviant finding was identified during the analysis that was not a neat fit for alienation theory. Just about all of the participants – and often spontaneously – noted that they also enjoyed social work. Rachel provides a typical example of this response: "I want to be a social worker. I sound so negative .... I do enjoy the work. I cannot imagine not being a social worker" (Rachel).

The classic interpretation of alienation is that it is a constant condition where the worker is instantly alienated in the workplace and beyond. Now that may be the case elsewhere (though that lies beyond the remit of this book) but a contradiction exists here. How can a worker be simultaneously alienated but still enjoy their work? This situation is where abductive inference is useful. Instead of rejecting the theory in its pure logical form it can be adapted, perhaps not for the theory as a whole, but definitely for this historical example of alienation. The compassionate self being such a deep part of the participants' identity does not immediately succumb to the travails and pressures of the workplace. Glimpses of its realization can be found in social work practice. The moments when the compassionate self is realized act as a countervailing tendency to the general tendency of alienation. They act as a form of compensation or, as Lordon (2014) would suggest, a moment of affect when capitalist labour returns an emotional as well as financial reward for willing servitude.

Those moments though are not constant and their compensatory presence, at least for the longer-serving social workers, diminished over time and the negative experiences became overwhelming. For the longer-serving participants, what Nathan called a "crash point" was reached. That was a critical moment when suddenly alienation was experienced at its sharpest. Here Sheila reflects on her crash point:

'When it came to going to my client after that I just couldn't face it. I broke down in tears and told my colleague I needed to go home. So, we returned to the office and I went home. I was then off after that. So that had been my actual breaking point.' (Sheila)

The crash point had considerable consequences for participants. Some were required to take leave of absences due to illness that they attributed to the negative impact that work had on their lives. While for others, and typically the longer served participants, a cynicism and weariness was evident. The contradiction between what they expected their labour would involve and the daily realities of social work proved difficult to resolve. Two older social workers, Bob and Sheila, talked of planning to retire earlier than anticipated. While for Nathan and for Richard, they had made the decision to reduce the centrality of work to their sense of self and focus on other aspects of life instead. As Richard noted, "You've got to refocus on what's more important: a job, in the end, is just a job." Their decisions must also be understood in the context of alienation theory. Choosing to compartmentalize their lives into separate spheres to prevent the travails of work overflowing into domestic life may seem a sensible solution.

Taking that action perhaps indicated that they had developed, in that classic trope of neoliberalism, resilience: dispositions and strategies to prevent negative reactions to potentially harmful external events. From the standpoint of alienation theory, while their agency may seem a protective move, it speaks of a fragmenting of the lifeworld, where labour is set aside as not being capable of providing the affirmation of self. Life, for Marx, should be lived as a totality where all experiences enrich existence and allow for the flourishing of talents and creativity. What Nathan and Richard were expressing here is human-nature alienation. They had become estranged from what had compelled them into social work in the first place.

Analysing the working experiences of social workers from the vantage point of alienation theory introduces: (1) new insights into the causes of the disillusionment and poor wellbeing experienced by social workers; and (2) suggests new solutions to those problems. Developing Lavalette's and Ferguson's (ibid) argument further, we can clearly see that the causes of disillusionment and poor wellbeing are not to be found in the failings and deficiencies of individual social workers. The causes are rather to be found in the objective relations and circumstances in which they work. Those relations are defined by the political objectives of governments pursuing a variety of neoliberal ideological projects. In the moment of work those relations lead to the loss of control experienced by the social worker. They are not free to realize their human nature in the form of the compassionate self. They become estranged from it as their labour is not working with people in need of help, but rather the technocratic and reductive reports that seek to rationalize and discipline the lifeworld of a service-user and the labour of a social worker.

To, therefore, offer a solution to this issue requires travelling beyond discourses and technologies of resilience, a familiar trope of neoliberalism that seeks to reinvent structural maladies as individual responsibility and is often raised as a response to any problem. In resilience discourses the social actor is encouraged to be constantly fluid and malleable, able to meet any challenge. The anthropology of resilience is one where the subject is imagined as possessing no history or, indeed, any form of human nature or emotional self. They are instead imagined as an endlessly flexible rational entity that coldly moves from meeting one challenge to the other (Dardot and Laval 2013). What this research indicates is that for these social workers adopting neoliberal forms of resilience would entail suppressing core aspects of their identities and what motivated them to become social workers in the first place, a heavy loss.

The solution that logically emerges from what I have been discussing here is for social workers to regain control over their labour process – a point also raised by Lavalette and Ferguson (2018). That would entail, for example, social workers being able to collectively decide what level of report writing is necessary, how funds are used, how much time to devote to working directly with service-users and which of their repertoire of skills to use. Given the current highly managerialist context of social work (Tsui and Cheung 2004), that goal may seem idealistic, but it is worth pointing out that social work has taken different forms over time. A re-engagement with some of the literature and ideas that were common currency in Harris' (2003) parochial professional period in the 1970s could be instructive. Mayer and Timms' (1970) classic, *The Client Speaks*, points to a radically different social work from that of today in the United Kingdom. What may be more problematic is how to arrive at that place. When asked what changes they would like to see in social work practice all the participants pointed to bureaucratic or procedural alterations. Nor did they see trade unionism as a vehicle for change.

Conclusion

The case study presented in this chapter illustrates how alienation can affect the wellbeing of a particular group of workers. In their discussions of work, their lives and their wellbeing, the lived experience of alienation begins to emerge. Alienation emerges not as singular homogeneous entity but one that is constituted by the relations of the workplace in connection to the labour process and what is produced, the historical circumstances forming their labour and how they actively make meaning in their work. As indicated in Chapter 1, alienation is a tendency within capitalism. That experience of alienation depends on what other relations of power or countervailing tendencies are at play at the time in that context.

The group of workers discussed would be classed as professionals, and their particular empirical experiences of alienation will not be the same as other groups of workers. Even though they felt they lacked autonomy in the labour process they can still exert more autonomy in their work than other workers. Experience of alienation will always possess a relative dimension, where the context and the contingent relations of a particular form of labour will shape the experiences of workers.

The movement between the theory and the empirical findings is important here. The theory guides the research, helping to frame what questions to ask and what lines of enquiry to pursue. The lines of enquiry focus on what is occurring in the labour process, what the workers' experiences and interpretations are, and the relations of control and power in their context. Similar questions can be posed concerning the object of labour, their relations with other workers and the exercise or otherwise of their capacities to be creative and how and if they find their labour enriching or estranging.

Copyright notice

5

Is Alienation Theory
Still Relevant?

Mike's story

"It's a great job but terrible work," said Mike. He worked for an online delivery service.

Mike loved his bike, loved cycling. If he wasn't out cycling, then he was repairing and tweaking his bike ensuring a smooth high performance ride every time he went out onto the city streets or beyond its boundaries and along country tracks. He knew that he needed work. He had to eat and his bike cost money to run. Working for an online platform delivery company was therefore a logical choice. It would allow him to earn money while cycling around the city. A perfect match.

At first it was fun. He soon found that there was a sort of workplace. Other cyclists, all early 20-something men like him, hung out at a central location in the city seated around a statue to some old king or other, waiting for the app to ping to provide them with the info for the next pickup and delivery. The camaraderie between them was energizing. They shared maintenance tips and tails of near mishaps and crashes. One guy had spilled off his bike while on a pizza delivery. Took a corner too fast and too tight in order to meet the designated time, skidded and then found himself painfully lying on the pavement. He contacted the delivery company through the app. Their concern was immediate: was the pizza okay? That brought a laugh, but the graze on his knee still hadn't quite healed.

As the weeks went by, the job wasn't what Mike hoped it to be. It was either frenetically hectic and full on or nothing at all. There was a lot of waiting. Too much waiting. Not all days were busy, sometimes Saturdays could be unexpectedly quiet. Sure, he could chat and banter with the other delivery cyclists. But it meant he wasn't on his bike. That was frustrating. Especially in the summer when it was dry, with long light nights, a time when he'd otherwise be out cycling.

Then again, when it was busy that could be frustrating too. Some nights it was constant, no time to stop or catch your breath. To help offset the pain in his knees he experienced at peak times, Mike loaded up as much as he could on painkillers and anti-inflammatory medication. The pain in his knees aside he felt fine. And anyway, the alternatives to this job were not great. Marek said it was better working in the kitchens of some of the takeaway chains or restaurants from where they collected their orders. That work looked awful. Trapped in a small hot room, being constantly told what to do and under constant pressure to perform faster.

In terms of the future he wasn't too sure what he would do when he was a little older. Perhaps he would get a proper job, a lot of the others said that too, but what is a proper job?

Alienation today

Penguin's covers for just about all of Marx's books in their catalogue adopt a classic 19th-century painting of early industrialization, or black-and-white plate photography from the same period. The Penguin edition of *Capital III*, published in 1992, features a picture of the mighty Krupp steam hammer, its scale overwhelming any of the factory workers working nearby, who only appear as anonymous blurs. The images on the books are part of a perspective to view Marx and his work as historic, as a depiction and analysis of the time in which he was living. The clear implication of which is to state his ideas no longer apply to contemporary capitalism as production in the 19th century concerned itself with metal bashing while in the 21st century it is centred around high-end tech and precarious work as exemplified by workers like Mike in the opening vignette. He is part of the shift to the platform economy. Instead of being an employee for a company, with all the few benefits that may bring, he is classed as an independent contractor, with very little independence, whose working time is controlled by an app.

The question arises is alienation a redundant concept? As Ricoeur (1968) observed, alienation is so semantically overridden it has become rendered meaningless. Or it has perhaps been superseded by concepts more capable of analysing the textures of contemporary capitalism, with its flows and relationships and formations of new subjectivities as discussed in previous chapters. As indicated from the outset I believe it is not redundant, and, in fact, the capitalism of the 21st century is as alienative as in previous periods of capitalism. Marxist geographer Harvey also shares this diagnosis. He makes the very bold statement that '[a]lienation exists almost everywhere' (Harvey 2018: 140). Work, he argues, has become increasingly meaningless. A similar diagnosis of work is made by Graeber (2018) that many jobs today are what he rhetorically terms 'bullshit jobs'. These are jobs void of any discernible meaning for the worker, nor do they seem to serve any societal good. These are jobs for jobs' sake, leading to corrosive resentment, and to a form of what I would say is other-human alienation, turning on people with jobs whose work could be interpreted as fulfilling in some way.

There are many ways to try and answer the question of continued relevance for alienation theory today. One way would be to seek out similarities between when Marx was writing with today to justify the relevance of the theory. Precarity, for example, is regarded as a feature of contemporary capitalism with the ubiquity of the gig economy and platform-based delivery services such as Deliveroo. Interest in this topic follows from the work of Standing (2011) and his identification of the 'precariat' as a distinct fraction within the working class.

Precarity, though, is nothing new within capitalism. It has always been a feature of work throughout the history of capitalism. Betti (2016) makes the useful point that we only think of precarity as a new development if we draw a contrast to a supposed golden age of Fordism. That perception of Fordism provides a norm for classifying and understanding what should be seen as work. The assumption of Fordism as the norm is questionable on several counts. First, Fordist working practices were never the norm in the global majority. Multiple different forms of labour process can be found globally that do not accord with the Fordist model.

The historian Rubenhold's (2019) corrective to the case of Jack the Ripper introduces the histories and identities of the women whom the Ripper murdered also reveals how easy it was for women, especially, but also men, to slip through the precarious cracks of Victorian society. She draws out not just the biography of the five women who were murdered but how their lives were shaped and conditioned by the structures of that period of capitalism, particularly the brutal interactions of class and gender. The women became vulnerable not through poor individual choices but because of the unforgiving structures of capitalism at that time. An employer could terminate employment at a whim, plunging the unfortunate worker and their family into misery and destitution.

Seeking out the similarities could be one way to claim the continued relevance of alienation. But doing so runs the risks of misunderstanding what Marx was attempting to achieve across all his work. Marx's whole project was not a description of Victorian capitalism. It was to isolate and bring to the fore at the purest level of abstraction the core relations and core logical forms of which capitalism comprises, and provides the dynamic by which it operates as a social and economic system. Nowhere is that more notable in Marx than in his famous description of the forward energy of capitalism in the *Communist Manifesto*:

> The bourgeoisie cannot exist without constantly revolutionising the instruments of production, and thereby the relations of production, and with them the whole relations of society. Conservation of the old modes of production in unaltered form, was, on the contrary, the first condition of existence for all earlier industrial classes. Constant

revolutionising of production, uninterrupted disturbance of all social conditions, everlasting uncertainty and agitation distinguish the bourgeois epoch from all earlier ones. All fixed, fast-frozen relations, with their train of ancient and venerable prejudices and opinions, are swept away, all new-formed ones become antiquated before they can ossify. (Marx and Engels 1998: 6)

Or, put more pithily and in contemporary Silicon Valley parlance, *move fast and break things*. Marx understood that capitalism is built on restless relations that can never be still, which need to be in flux and flow. His futurology in *The Fragment of Machines* has been interpreted by various writers, such as Hardt and Negri (2009) and Lazzarato (1996), as providing a glimpse into a world where knowledge becomes a productive force as it is today.

Jameson (2010) provides a useful metaphor for what Marx was seeking to do in his work by discovering and laying out at the highest level of abstraction the core relations with capitalism. Picasso's *Young Girl Throwing a Rock* painted in 1931 is typical of the artist's work. The surreal image is in no way a lifelike image of a girl throwing a rock. But it contains all the elements necessary for the viewer to perceive a young cis-female throwing a stone. Picasso here is not trying to represent a concrete historical moment, a single young woman throwing a stone on a particular day. He is instead trying to communicate the core elements that make up a young girl throwing a stone, so when we see an actual young woman acting in history we can perceive what is happening. That was Marx's mission in his work, what are the core elements of capital, what are its logics, the core relations. He was stripping away all the contingent relations, the noise and distortion, the misleading minutia to distil down what is absolutely necessary for capitalism to exist. That point is why *Capital* begins with a discussion of the commodity. By understanding the commodity, Marx identifies the basic cell or elementary form of capitalism, and crucially what makes capitalist society different from other social formations. All human societies make things, objects that serve a purpose, or use value, but those objects operate in a way that is different from a commodity in capitalist society. Recall the example of Muisca society mentioned in Chapter 3 in explaining the relationships between human agency and the agency of matter. The intricate gold statuettes were a common social product, one that symbolized a religious belief system. The statuettes were not produced to sell to acquire other objects.

It is the selling of objects as commodities that makes capitalism distinctive as social and historical form. The objects that social agents create are produced with the intention of selling, therefore acquiring an exchange value and becoming a commodity. A commodity still retains a use value, that it possesses some purpose that is useful. It doesn't matter whether that use is for 'the stomach or from fancy', as Marx puts it, all that matters is that some use can be found. So, by beginning his analysis of capitalism by focusing on the commodity he is beginning to unlock all the necessary relations that power capitalism, the core relations that constitute its essence.

Therefore, the task of applying Marx's work is not to hark back in time but to apply his theories to the present and move between the pure abstractions of the theory and the historical present. Ollman (2003) stresses the importance of relations (*Verhältnis*) within Marx's overall philosophy and ontology. He identifies that Marx builds his worldview using a philosophy of internal relations where all objects are fundamentally connected with each other. Saying that objects exist in a relationship with each other may seem an obvious point. That perspective is the basis of much positivist science where *x* exerts an influence on *y*. Marx proceeds further than just simply noting that certain objects are related to each other and can exert an effect on another object. What he claims is that objects come into being through their relations, that the relations are internally constitutive of that object, the relation is crucially not just contingent but necessary for an object to exist. So, therefore, unlike Kant who held objects as being a thing-in-itself (*Ding-an-Sich*) that could never be fully comprehended, for Marx objects can be understood by the various relations of which are they comprised.

The transitive and intransitive dimensions of knowledge

One further way to make the case for alienation is through how knowledge is created and reproduced. Just because a concept of a theory falls from grace, is no longer a staple of sociological discussion and research, does not logically entail that the phenomena it sought to understand has disappeared. Bhaskar (1975) draws attention to the transitive and intransitive dimensions of knowledge. A temporal difference exists between the two dimensions. The second domain, the intransitive, exists ontologically prior to the first. It is there whether social agents are consciously aware of it or not. It is the phenomena under study and comprises of the various relations that make it what it is. Its presence can be detected in regularities of its actualization, of it having some form of affect that is objectively present. The first dimension, the transitive, is the activity of social agents, how they research, theorize and conceptualize the phenomena. The transitive dimension can be fluid, constantly changing as interpretations of the intransitive domain alter due to increased empirical knowledge or, as happens in the social sciences, new frames of theory emerge that interpret the intransitive differently.

Bhaskar's (1975) understanding of knowledge is radically different from that of the post-modernist orthodoxy that has dominated sociology over the last few decades. For him – and those in the critical realist tradition, such as Sayer (2000) – they reject the post-modernist assertion that it is human activity that creates reality, for them the intransitive dimension is purely a discourse lacking any reality, whatever reality may be. There is not the space to enter a full critique of post-modernism. I flag instead the main objections posed by others for brevity. By the way, I have always struggled to fully define post-modernism, it seems to spawn as many interpretations as alienation.

Of late, within that transitive dimension of knowledge, a re-engagement with alienation theory is occurring. I wrote in 2011 that a process of remembering, of re-engaging with alienation theory was evident (Yuill 2011). I noted at that point in time several academics drawing on alienation and that wave has travelled further since then. At the beginning of this chapter, I cited Harvey and his clear statement that alienation permeates global society. He is not the only one. Jaeggi (2014) has provided a substantial philosophical treatment of alienation. Her work sought to overcome the paternalistic and overly essentialist versions of alienation theory that have existed. I have drawn on her work earlier in this book and she provides a way forward out of those problems. Other substantial contributions have been provided by Tenhouten (2017), who highlights the role of affect within alienation. At other points in this book I have drawn on contributions by Musto (2010), Zoubir (2018), Stuart et al (2013), Øversveen (2022) and others. Reichle and Bescherer (2021) have applied alienation to housing studies and how alienation can result in a negative solidarity between residents. Musto (2021) has also released a major book covering the uses of alienation throughout the work of Marx, demonstrating that, *contra* Althusser, alienation was not simply a dalliance by a young humanist romantic.[1]

Tourism studies provides another interesting line of studies into alienation. Not a surprise, as MacCannell (1976) was drawing on Marxian alienation theory in the Golden Age of alienation studies in the 1960s and 1970s. His concern was with the reasons why people seek authentic experiences (whatever that may be) in response to the inauthenticity of their alienated lives. The influence of Marxian alienation studies still persist. But as Xue et al (2014) note, more contemporary research on tourism and alienation is theorized from different sources, augmenting or using Marx as a reference point for other perspectives on alienation. Existentialist approaches are common, with alienation regarded as an inescapable condition of modern life (for example, Wang 1999), while Vidon (2019) seeks out Lacan to explain the psychological experience of alienation and authenticity.

Overall, a vibrant array of work on alienation exists in the early decades of the 21st century. That is not to make any rash claims that the study of alienation has reclaimed the position it once held within social science during the Golden Era in the 1960s and 1970s. It simply has not. But a growing

---

[1] Unfortunately for me, and given the pandemic period in which I have been writing, Musto's book was released too late in the day for me to incorporate into my discussion.

interest and re-engagement is evident. Once a focus on alienation begins to appear regularly in leading sociology journals then it might be time to confirm a full return. How this emerging interest in alienation develops will be interesting. So far, it is beginning to demonstrate some of the strains and tensions present in the Golden Age literature. Philosophers and empiricists do not seem to draw from each other's work. If alienation studies are not to replicate the pitfalls of the past then dialogue is required between theory and research.

There has been one contribution to the study of alienation that requires a little more attention due to its higher profile than the other works that I have mentioned. Lordon makes interesting points about alienation that are useful, but I do not agree with the full extent of his thesis.

Lordon draws on the materialist philosophy of Spinoza which he combines with the historical materialism of Marx. Varying degrees of combining Marx and Spinoza are nothing new – think of the various combined or solo works produced by Hardt and Negri for instance (Hardt and Negri 2000, 2005, 2009). As Duhe (2017), following Casarino (2011), notes, Lordon offers a much deeper synthesis of the two than found elsewhere. Lordon's rationale for doing so stems not from thinking that there is a hidden Spinozist influence in Marx that requires uncovering, but that Marx does not allow for desire or affect to play a role in the cycles of capital accumulation and exploitation of workers. Spinoza fills that gap. His argument is that desire for specific emotional states that can be realized as part of the labour process motivates social agents to work within the exploitative assemblages of capitalism.

Spinoza's concept of the conatus is central to Lordon's work. The conatus animates and mobilizes human existence, providing the energy that fuels striving to be and to act in the world, to do the best to survive. Williams (2010: 247) understands the conatus as a 'generative force' that 'pulsates through living forms'. The conatus is a fundamental of Spinoza's materialism where he posits human beings as embodied entities with no separation between mind and body, which forms part of his wider critique of Descartes' dualist philosophy. Humans are instead assemblages of emotions, feelings, anatomy, biological and neurological processes and so on, all of which exist simultaneously and in relation with each other but also with the society in which the social agent lives.

The conatus becomes manifest through desire: one of the three main affects in Spinoza's anthropology. Spinoza (1996: 104) understands desire to be 'man's very essence'. What a social agent desires shapes who they are and figures in the choices that they make in life. As such desire becomes an integral element in the morphology of Spinozist subjectivity. No prefigured subject exists for Spinoza, and by extension for Lordon. Subjectivity emerges instead in the specific history of an individual's lifecourse and is formed by lifetime experiences and memories, or as Lordon puts it (2012: 16), 'over the long course of (social) biographical trajectories'. It is these experiences and memories that give rise to an individual's particular desires. The origins of which are therefore external in origin, without any recourse to some form of essentialist self. Desire develops through experience in relation to a distinct object (or objects) that the individual associates with the two other affects that Spinoza identifies: joy or sadness. Acquiring an object of desire results in a joyful affect that adds energy (*potentia*) and additional drive to the conatus or improves wellbeing and the ability to survive and thrive. Not acquiring that object results in sadness which exerts the opposite effect and finishes the ability to thrive. Desire therefore gains analytic primacy in understanding why social agents act in particular ways. It becomes an object to be sought and identified in the data as it unlocks the motives and reasoning of the social agent and, ultimately, what determines their actions.

Critically though, social agents do not simply follow their desires unrestrained and with no recourse to anything else. The subject does not exist as itself. It exists within a relation of other things and within vectors of power that place limits on the fluidity of desire. Desire is therefore not free range, roaming unbidden, but is contained and channelled in a matrix of different relations that pre-exist and exist around the subject. As Williams (2017: np) notes of Lordon, his 'analysis helps to explain how relations of power combine or hold a nominally dispersed or mutative subjectivity in a static position (of domination or servitude), whilst offering an example of how dispositions, habits and beliefs are a function of material practice'.

Different phases of capitalism hold subjectivity static in different ways. Neoliberalism achieves that state with the co-linearity of the desires of the employee and the employer. The more the desires of the worker align with the master desire of the capitalist then the greater the desire for submitting to servitude. But not just submitting to capital but actively and consciously giving as much of oneself in the job. In modern capitalism the capitalist must therefore make sure that alongside the material reproduction of labour there is also the affective reproduction of labour. The capitalist needs to maintain the joy, or at least offer moments of joy, to ensure the continuation of servitude.

The trick played by neoliberal capitalism, according to Lordon, is to offer a joyful resolution both to the desire to earn money – it still remains essential for material, social and biological reproduction – but also that there will be some aspect of labour that will be joyful: 'If employees accept the enlistment relation imposed on them by the social structure of capitalism, and submit to demands for ever-rising productivity, it is not only the effect of compulsion or organisational violence, but also because at times they get something out of it: opportunities for joy' (Lordon 2014: 28). So, what do we take, what do we reject? I agree with Fleming that Lordon makes too strong a case for affect being central to the workplace and for capital buying off working-class resistance by dropping in the occasional moment of joy. As Fleming (2015: 84) stridently notes, '[m]anagement today has no interest in whether you like or love it (although it would like you to think it does). And it certainly does not like itself. General happiness is not its concern; nor are lasting social bonds'. Jaffe (2021: 12), in her critique of work, says the same: 'Work, after all, has no feelings. It cannot love.'

In some forms of labour that may be the case. Think of the social workers I discussed in Chapter 4. Evidence existed there of affect playing a role in their labour, their desire, in the Spinozist sense, to work with others and the occasional moment when that desire was, albeit fleetingly, realized. I feel that emotions emerge from the human nature I sketched out earlier, that wanting to help others and enjoying the camaraderie of other workers form the affective terrain of work and the emotions that the structures of capitalism alienate and estrange. I am also wary of Lordon's outright rejection of essentialism. As I tried to argue in Chapter 2, some form of embodied human nature needs to exist, but his insights into how affects develop in an individual biography are useful in explaining some why some workers may agree to capitalist servitude.

Neoliberalism as a machine of alienation?

What if we also search for sources of alienation in contemporary neoliberal capitalism? Neoliberalism is a particular form of capitalism, though one that evades easy definition. For Brenner et al (2010: 182), neoliberalism is a 'rascal concept – promiscuously pervasive, yet inconsistently defined, empirically imprecise and frequently contested'. Its surface gloss never matches its practice in the real world. Freedom is often advanced by its intellectual supporters, but for many social agents neoliberalism is experienced as stark authoritarianism in the form of constant metrics, measurement and forms of surveillance.

Neoliberalism emerges historically for distinct reasons as Harvey (2007) sets out in his analysis of neoliberalism. On one hand, the embedded liberalism, where the private sector existed alongside state ownership and a raft of government regulation, that had evolved post-Second World War was starting to fail. The 1973 embargo by the Organisation of the Petroleum Exporting Countries is often touted as the moment that the post-war Keynesian consensus comes unstuck, but it was already in poor shape at the tail end of the 1960s. Stagflation, a combination of stagnant growth and high inflation, was a persistent feature of the time, wreaking havoc on European and Northern American economies. As Harvey (2005) notes, why neoliberalism emerged as currently dominant is not clear. Its ascendancy was far from sure at the time. But the Mont Pelerin Society had been busy in the background, laying down the intellectual foundations of neoliberalism. It was a collection of academics, Hayek and Friedson were leading lights within this grouping, funded by corporate interests and who sought to influence government policy. The common bond between the different members of the Society was an antipathy to any form of government control or collectivist policy.

It was not just communism or socialism that they hated but also the regulatory capitalism advocated by Keynes. Their direction of travel was for the state to be re-tooled away from its regulatory or redistributive function, as had been the case under embedded liberalism and Keynesian economics, to act as the creator and protector of the free market. In practice, this change of direction meant nullifying any opposition to the free market. Organized labour was the main target in the initial phases of a nation state imposing neoliberal policies on its population. During the 1980s Regan in the United States took on the air traffic controllers, while at the same time Thatcher decided that the National Union of Miners were the 'enemy within', laying siege to working-class mining communities across England, Scotland and Wales. I have already mentioned in an earlier chapter the murderous imposition of neoliberalism in Chile following the Pinochet coup in 1973 against the democratically elected Allende government, but the historical point that neoliberalism did not enter the world as pure, unsullied economic theory always needs repeating. It comes wrapped in destruction, barbarism and brutalization.

As Dardot and Laval (2013) argue, there is a misunderstanding that neoliberalism seeks to eradicate the state, that it is another version of anti-statist classical liberalism. They assert that the mission of neoliberalism is to recast the state as (1) the entrepreneurial state that exercises an activist role in both creating and sustaining the market relations; and (2) acts to discipline the population so as to maintain the running of the market and the creation of neoliberal subjectivities. Both points emerge because as Dardot and Laval (2013) argue free markets are not spontaneous entities but need to be brought into existence without any barrier to their existence or threat to their continuation and it is the duty of the neoliberal state to remove barriers and potential threats to the flourishing of free markets. Mirowski (2013) makes a similar point concerning the constructivist nature of free markets and that for neoliberals the state needs to be remade and re-tasked in order to create the terrain in which markets can operate.

A level of duplicity also exists within neoliberalism. On one hand its intellectual exponents centre freedom as its aim for society. But it is a very limited and narrow form of freedom. It is not the freedom for employees to collectively organize their work how they want to do it, it is not about relating to others as equals. It is, instead, the freedom for a small economic elite to accumulate greater levels of profit without what they would regard as regulatory restraint such as workers' rights or environmental protection. A brutal unforgiving heart beats at the centre of Hayek. As Filip (2012: 74) notes of Hayek when comparing him to Polanyi, ' he was of the opinion that freedom had nothing to do with achieving equality in people's skills, capacities, incomes, and wealth'. Hayek's vision of the free market is an exercise in idealism, that cannot comprehend that the supposed infallible free market operates without producing any harms. He elides the obvious problem that any society is not a level playing field, and the sorting mechanism of the free market favours those who by their structural position possess multiple advantages bestowed by their economic, social and cultural capitals.

Neoliberalism also operates on more insidious levels in the workplace, where it seeks to create a form of subjectivity that is different from the Fordist subjectivity of the production line. It advances its own theory of human nature. All humans are naturally individualistic and self-maximizing (translation: greedy) posited as *Homo economicus*. The individual social gent becomes the author of their own future and destiny. More importantly, they are also posited as a restless engine of activity or wanting to add to their lives, more success, greater income and so on. The neoliberal subject is the lone agent developing strategies that will achieve those aims. The collective drops out of sight.

In the medical sociology literature we see how neoliberalism's centring of aggressive individualism results in a responsibilization, a move that depoliticizes the problems of society, shifting blame onto the victim. Pirie (2016) provides a useful example of responsibilization in relation to disordered eating. Social life is saturated with invitations for the overconsumption of food, with a normalization of historically unprecedented portion sizes. The fast-food industry is a prime mover for the increase in calorie-heavy meals. But as people begin to eat more and obesity increases the cause of obesity is not centred on the food industry but on the individual. It is their fault that they are overweight. As Williams and Annandale (2020) found in their research on how people try to lose weight, discourses of responsibilization result in stigma, anxiety and poor wellbeing.

Neoliberalism works in many ways to produce alienation. Some of which are more obvious than others. On one level it does so by reducing control that workers can exert over the labour process. A literature exists that covers what has been described as the 'new management', though now just normal management, introduced new modalities of management that witnesses micro-control over every aspect of the labour process.

The reduction of control over the labour process is not only experienced in routine or semi-skilled occupations. It is experienced across all occupations. Professional occupations are subject to increasing metrics of power that superficially make claims of quality and accountability but serve to further deepen managerial control. As Dardot and Laval state, the impulse to evaluate does allow for greater managerial control, but also goes much deeper in attempting to transform what it is to be a professional within the public sector:

> Measuring performance has become the elementary technology of power relations in public services. ... It tends to shape the activity itself and aims to produce subjective changes in the 'evaluated', so they meet their 'contractual commitments' to higher bodies. This involves reducing the autonomy acquired by a number of professional groups, such as doctors, judges and teachers, who are deemed to be expensive, lax or unproductive, by imposing on them the criterion of results constructed by a proliferating expert technostructure. (Dardot and Laval 2013: 250)

Another alienating tendency within neoliberal capitalism is the exhortation to always be working and to commodify all aspects of existence. Work becomes all. And it is not the form of labour that leads to self-realization and a feeling of completeness that I argued is a necessary part of human nature. Indeed, as Deleuze (1992) has argued, neoliberalism is about constant addition, that the social agent can no longer achieve a sense of completion, one always *has to be* doing more and more. And what you do engage in is never enough. The frantic pursuit of doing more is not the decision of the social agent, but inhered into what he calls a control society that disciplines by constantly moving the finishing line as opposed to telling you what to do. Ho (2009), in her ethnography of Wall Street traders, identifies how the culture of constant work emerges in the finance houses and banks in Wall Steet during the early 2000s. Traders were obliged to work absurd 90–100 hour weeks with any sign of not always working, such as grabbing only a few hours of sleep per day, regarded as weakness and cause for dismissal. The insidious effect of these trading areas is that the culture moves beyond Wall Street and corrodes other forms of work, creating a society where work is the dominant totality of existence.

This impulse is also evident in exhortations on social media to make the most of the day by waking at 5am, and then engaging in several exercises and practices that supposedly lead to self-improvement and self-betterment. Other social media memes make the claim that all people share the same 24 hours in the day, so if Beyoncé or Elon Musk can become rich and successful, then so can anyone. It is up to you how you use your time, after all you can turn your hobby into a side hustle. With laser focus on gaining new skills then a fortune is within reach. Neoliberalism therefore calls for constant work, constant devotion to exploiting every aspect of the self, emotions, bodies, talents, creativity, in the pursuit of goals that can never be realized: an ultimate form of alienation.

Conclusion

Is alienation still with us today? The answer is a firm yes. What I have argued is we need to think that alienation is not fixed to a certain historical period and only refers to some stereotypical image of a male worker on some Fordist production line. What matters are the social relations, and are they still alienating? The fundamental relations that Marx sought to identify throughout his work are still in operation and the relationship between capital and workers persists. It just takes different historical forms. The intransitive condition has not changed, and it appears that the transitive domain, what academics write about, is witnessing a return to discussing alienation in some form or other.

We also live in a neoliberal society. This form of capitalism is highly alienating. It further reduces control of the labour process introducing a mass of surveillance and control techniques to ensure compliance and limiting the creativity of the worker. But neoliberalism also strikes at what it is to be human. It attempts to create a social agent that exceeds the conventional boundary of the *Homo economicus*. The neoliberal citizen is one who devotes their life to work in a never-ending search for profit and commodification of all aspects of existence.

6

Beyond Alienation?

In the preceding chapters I have outlined that alienation exerts a toll on wellbeing and health. Human lives are stunted and damaged and, stepping into a more normative register, they are not what they could be. The capacities and capabilities that social agents possess lack the freedom to be fully actualized, and when those capacities and capabilities are enacted, it is within a set of estranged relations for the purposes of capitalist accumulation.

So, what can we do? What can we do to move to a social formation where this does not occur, where social agents can realize and enact their potential?

One theme that runs throughout this book is that alienation emerges out of multiple social relationships particular to capitalism. It is not a given, a fixed natural state of affairs that we must simply endure without complaint as that is the natural order. Alienation like so many other social constructed inequalities is not an inevitable or natural part of existence. On a very high level of abstraction, it is an instance of social construction, albeit one with a very powerful weight of material force behind it. That means the relations and circumstances that produce alienation can be changed. New relations can be created that could either dramatically reduce alienation or dispense with it altogether.

Time for a new society?

In sociological parlance the causes of alienation are structural. A host of research and theorization has attested that how social structures have come into being leads to highly deleterious effects on health and wellbeing. The relationship between ethnicity and wellbeing provides a useful example. One common experience for racialized minority groups living in majority White countries is worse health and wellbeing in comparison with the majority population. Older research in this area lapsed into victim blaming, holding people of colour to account for shorter life expectancy and poorer health during life. Everything from the deficits of traditional food culture to genetics were mobilized to place the blame. However, a new wave of research in this area found that the reasons why racialized minority groups experience worse health are located in the racist structures of society. Racism affects the lives of racialized groups in multiple ways. Access to social, material and culture resources such as housing, access to employment, promotion at work are denied alongside deeper denials of the legitimacy of an ethnic group's heritage identity and recognition within a society. All of these spring from the construction of racism across time, which crystallized during the North Atlantic slave trade as a legitimating ideology for the forced enslavement and the murder of millions of people from West Africa and other people who became colonized subjects in European empires. So, if the life expectancy and overall wellbeing of racialized people is to improve then it is not down to focusing on individual behaviours, but rather to look at how racism and the legacies of colonialism can be undone within a society.

Therefore, to ensure that life for millions of people is less alienating, a move to some other form of social arrangement is required. That is a very grand statement. It also raises a number of issues and problems. One of which is another objection to alienation theory, that it smuggles in a paternalistic ideology of what life should be. This point was already touched on when discussing the Frankfurt School. In the analysis of alienation and wider social malaise developed by Marcuse and Adorno an elitist or paternalistic vision of society has been identified that is critical of popular culture for being a false ideology that draws attention away from the underlying exploitation of capitalism. As was discussed in relation to human nature, an essence does exists, is present, but it is one that is based on the potential of human capacities, of change movement and transformation. It is not one where humans return to some form of technophobic pre-Lapsarian ideal. For a start, when would that point in time be? Referring again to Graeber and Wengrow (2021) here really was no perfect time of humanity before it all went completely wrong. A post-capitalist society would not be one of placing the gears into reverse, where, for instance, we would abandon all technology in favour of turning the clock back to some mythic past.[1]

Marx famously never really laid out what a future socialist society or a society where alienation was at least reduced would look like, beyond a few comments about spending half the day working and the rest engaged in leisure pursuits, such as hunting and shooting, referring to the main leisure activities of his time. The lack of any programme of a future society was a wise move by Marx. He recognized that capital is a constantly evolving and

---

[1] This is not to denigrate craft work as recommended by Sennett (2008), by any means at all. The labour people engage with in a post-capitalist society will be meaningful and rewarding. It will be engaged with on the basis of self-fulfilment rather than exploitation.

changing set of relations. Any speculation on what a future society could be like is based on what is possible at the point in time in which the speculation is made. It also needs to take into account the specifics of place.

Had I written this book in 1990, the vast power of the internet and other digital technologies was still science fiction, and the ability of this to improve people's lives would not have been apparent. I certainly do not advocate any return to a mythic pre-capitalist past. In fact, that, to me, cuts against what Marx was wanting a new society to be like. He saw a future society that takes the best from what is present as the old capitalist society begins to collapse and social agents 'set free the elements of the new society with which old collapsing bourgeois society itself is pregnant' (Marx 1974: 213).

One example of freeing elements within current society is provided by Bastani (2019). He calls for the future to be one of fully automated luxury communism, where technology makes possible a post-work society where humans (or rather post-humans) are freed up from the drudgery of the waged-labour with machines doing all the work. Technologies such as 3-D printing, wind and solar power, genetic editing and synthetic foods could therefore allow social agents to actualize their capacities and capabilities. Some level of labour will be required, that is undeniable, but the majority of the time will be available for what makes life matter. Bastani also believes that a luxurious communist future of surplus will solve other issues societies face. A move to renewable energies and other forms of food will help to tackle climate change.

Though he does not touch on alienation, the society that Bastani evokes is one where the causes of alienation would be either absent or greatly reduced. For example, in this society production is geared towards need not profit.

Bastani is not alone in wishing to repurpose technology for the betterment of humanity. Dyer-Witheford (2009: np), in his calls for what he calls biocommunism, also acknowledges that a future society would use technology to extend the capacities and capabilities of humanity. The following extract from a conference presentation he gave captures well the point that I am trying to make, that a post-capitalist society is about creating a new and novel version of humanity:

> Can we think, even start to think, a communism adequate to these conditions, something we might call a *biocommunism*? The gamble of Marxism is that liberation lies through, not prior to, alienation. There can be no return to earth, only the recapture of the strange planet to which capital has abducted us. A species-being politics cannot adhere to a fixed image of the human. It should rather admit mutation, evolutions that spring new senses and extensions, but on the condition that this is a mass transit, a collective reappropriation of the powers privately expropriated in the planet factory. It cannot be a crusade to

save humanity (or nature) as it is, or was, or is supposed to have once been. But nor can it be a self-annihilatory surrender to the delirium of techno-capital. A politics of species-being would instead be a struggle to intensify tendencies to socialization and commonality implicit in the new forces of production and destruction. High technologies such as digital networks and genetic engineering are species-level projects. In the social cooperation required for their production, the scale of their implementation, and their collective consequences, they tend to what Marx termed 'communal activity, and communal mind'. (Dyer-Witheford 2009: np)

Returning to Bastani: on one level he provides an interesting blueprint for the near future. He provides an excellent thought experiment on how society could be based on existing features of society. It is not a wild flight of the imagination. I am all for it. Though he does not specifically spell out how that change could be made. All of what he proposes could actually be enacted now and we could be in that world of machines assisting in making life more fulfilling and complete not just for humans but for other species on this planet too. The need is there, and the technology already exists. But yet, what seems a very easy case of joining point A with point B cannot be realized. I think how we achieve fully automated luxury communism is a slight weakness in Bastani's thesis. How we get to a luxurious future is unclear and underdeveloped.

But that kind of weakness is common to other visions of the future or how society could be transformed into a more equitable assemblage of relations. I made a similar critique of Nussbaum. The capabilities and capacities she outlines are highly desirable and a world where those capacities and capabilities could be realized and enacted in everyday life would be a giant leap forward on what we have now. It is moving to change that is difficult. One issue with technology, and it is irrelevant if that technology is a 3-D printer or a Krupp steam hammer, is the societal context in which it exists. Technology as part of capitalism is not there to make the lives of workers easier. It is there as part of the valorization of profit, dead labour taking control of living labour. As Wendling (2011) reminds us, Marx often describes machinery in *Capital* in very negative terms. Machines join the bestiary present within his writings of cyclops, werewolves and vampires. Machines are monstrous. They exist to extract further surplus rather than liberate workers and where machinery replaces worker, it is at the expense of the worker. The appearance of the microworker (or on-demand digital labour) on platforms such as Amazon Mechanical Turk provides an indication of how technology works for capital but against the interests of the worker. In that formation of labour work is highly precarious with little or no protection or job security. Microworkers are very much at the whim of what are termed requesters, those who outsource work (Webster 2016). Though not using the framework of alienation, this comment from a microworker in research by Panteli et al[2] illustrates a form of other-human alienation: 'I am a skilled and intelligent worker ... I am a human being, not an algorithm, and yet Requesters seem to think I am there just to serve their bidding. They do not respect myself and my fellow Turkers with a fair wage' (Panteli et al 2020: 485).

Trying to move towards a new less alienating society will not be an easy task. Think back to how neoliberalism was introduced. It was not through polite and logical arguments. It was through violence as detailed in Chapter 5. Capital will not give up its ascendancy easily. Even if capitalism is not a great state, lurching from one crisis to another, which must now include bio-crises such as COVID-19 or the next inherent structural crisis, the alternative may not be a default socialism. As Streeck (2016) contends, a world without capitalism may be a hellhole. He argues that capitalism is so embedded in every aspect of human existence that its collapse would lead to catastrophe. We would be left with a world with a blighted environment, ruled by oligarchs, with very little provision of welfare for that vast majority of people who would require it.[3]

Mark Fisher (2009, 2014, 2017, 2018, 2020) was developing an interesting and exciting analysis of what needs be done to provide possible new futures. His project was cut short by his untimely death. In his varied writings that drew on an eclectic range of literature and popular culture, in which horror writer Lovecraft rubs shoulders with Marx, alongside the weird and spectacular characters who populate the post-industrial landscapes of the songs of Mark E. Smith and The Fall, he tried to get to grips with capitalist realism. That concept is his main contribution to progressive thought. Capitalist realism refers to the dominance of capitalism in all spheres of the lifeworld, its greatest victory is to imprison thinking in the cell of 'there are no alternatives'. For Fisher, capitalist realism, 'is more like a pervasive atmosphere, conditioning not only the production of culture but also the regulation of work and education, and acting as a kind of invisible barrier constraining thought and action' (Fisher 2017). Acts of imagination for Fisher become political, hence his preoccupation with weird fiction, daring to think differently becomes the raw fuel for seeing beyond what, otherwise, would be a miserable despairing existence, where young people, in particular, are

---

[2]   Panteli et al's (2020) research also indicates that countervailing tendencies exist that may dimmish the isolation and atomization experienced by microworkers, such as taking collective action to further control over their labour process.

[3]   As Tooze (2017) notes in a review of Streeck, the alternative he provides is a left-Gaullist nationalism protectionism, which for Tooze raises more questions than it answers.

affected by hedonic melancholia – a constant search for happiness that only results in fleeting ephemeral affects.

There were two tracks, I feel, in Fisher's project. One was to outline how capitalist realism places limitations on possible futures, as outlined in the previous paragraphs. Anything other than the continuation of neoliberal capital as business as usual is not just forbidden but rendered impossible to imagine: the future is cancelled. The other was to draw together a bricolage of different ways of thinking about reality. It is the Situationist maxim of 'all power to the imagination', a necessary tonic for seeing through the confines of capitalist realism. It is essential to do so in order to break what Fisher regarded as one of the main achievements of contemporary capitalism to reduce the horizons of life to the capital wage labour relationship. To me, his work speaks to a deep alienation where social agents are alienated from each other, existence is fragmented and atomized, and where humans are alienated from their creativity to think about how much better life could be. Capitalist realism's greatest success is the shutting down of the human essences outlined earlier in this book. Capitalism no longer allows for the thinking through of alternatives. As Reed says of neoliberalism, capital no longer controls thoughts by burning books but by reducing the attention span of social agents so they lack the concentration to even read books. By re-engaging the imagination then the confines of capitalist realism can be breached. That is why he advocates an acid communism.

It was near to the end of his life that Fisher began to sketch out before his untimely death what he meant by acid communism, and, as such, it remains a never fully realized project. The following is the closest he gets to a definition:

> The concept of acid communism is a provocation and a promise. It is a joke of sorts, but one with very serious purpose. It points to something that, at one point, seemed inevitable, but which now appears impossible: the convergence of class consciousness, socialist-feminist consciousness-raising and psychedelic consciousness, the fusion of new social movements with a communist project, an unprecedented aestheticisation of everyday life. (Fisher 2022)

What, I believe, Fisher means by acid communism is not so much an outcome but a process of change. Central to that process are imagining different futures beyond what neoliberal capitalism now offers, thinking that life can be something other than the estranged fragmentation and atomization social agents currently endure. However, it is not a form of idealism, whereby thinking about a different future creates that future. He is clear that material activity must be simultaneously undertaken too, action on the streets and in the workplaces is all part of what is required to energize a better tomorrow. Fisher's inspiration is Cowie's (2012) analysis of how the optimism and hope of cultural and workplace radicalism of the 1960s in the United States degenerated into the splintered and fragmented 1970s. The 1960s and early 1970s witnessed gains for the working class and other oppressed groups throughout the Global North. As discussed earlier, France was edged towards a revolutionary situation, but the main gains for many workers were in pay, good working conditions and a more equal distribution of wealth. It is the America before the rustbelt appeared and opioids began claiming the lives of former workers and their families.

Central to Cowie's analysis is a tantalizing picture of how counterculture and working-class union organization, led from the ground up, very nearly combined and fused together to create a movement that possessed a vision of a possible future and the means by which that future could be achieved. However, the embedded conservativism of the union movement blocked that meeting of the power of the imagination and the industrial of power of workers from coming together.

Some of what Fisher calls for chimes with, I feel, Lordon (2014). He offers his prescription of moving towards a better society. He talks of realigning affects away from the labour process, de-fixating them and attaching affects and passions to new objects. This perspective emerges from his analysis that alienation is to some extent voluntary, it comes from within, as social agents find some form of happiness in work. I agree that he is correct in many regards, capitalism does enlist affects and emotions and then fixates them onto a very narrow range of objects and experiences within the workplace and everyday life. I do not agree, however, with his critique of essentialism, but he has recently raised an interesting point concerning how change could come about. Lordon (2022) has called for the removal of the sovereignty of capital, and to remake the institutions and the constitutions that are part-and-parcel of societies fit the needs and desires of workers, to provide a different range of affects that transcend the servitude of capitalism. As Toscano (2022) says of Lordon, he is attempting to raise the idea of a communist realism that any radical change requires to be rooted in the art of the possible, that workers will still work but for a different purposes. To that end, we must, he argues, overcome the weaknesses of the Occupy Movement that offered visions of a new society, new forms of collectivity but offered no programme for change and the weaknesses of Podemos, that offered programmatic change but no real vision of a new society, resulting in its absorption into the institutions that it set out to oppose. As he said in an earlier interview with *Il Manifesto*:

Putting an end to the empire of capital, which is a constitutionalized empire, you have to create a new constitution. A constitution that abolishes private ownership of the means of production and establishes

125

fitness for use: the means of production belonging to those who use them and those who use them doing things that are not for the development of capital. (Fana 2016: np)

In both sets of ideas we encounter questions rather than answers of how to change capital in all its complexity, move on from previous defeats and think about new forms of change so that we can move to a different society. These debates and discussions though have to be qualified as located in the Global North. Movements that seek change do so in a specific context given by history and solutions flow from that context.

All I am going to offer here are some what I call everyday-solidarities. I have no illusions that the everyday-solidarities suggested here are the rush and the push of the revolutionary moment and will somehow form an aggregate of activity that will magically transform our society. It will take something more than that to offer substantial change.

Everyday-solidarities perform two functions. The first is aligned to Fisher's analysis of capitalist realism, micro-solidarities are small moments of where the atomization of society, the fragmenting of humans into individuated competitive entities are disrupted and temporarily overcome. The second is to make life more bearable for other people, though they are not a permanent solution.

Everyday solidarities

'Make way for the worker'

'Make way for the worker' was a phrase I heard frequently used by the old Communist Party comrades, Spanish Civil War veterans, that I mentioned in the Preface, who I met in Aberdeen Trades Council way back in the 1980s. They said the phrase when we potentially interrupted someone going about their work. Sometimes it was a cleaner mopping the Trades Council sticky burgundy linoleum floor, or if we were on the street campaigning against whatever it was we were campaigning against at the time: if someone was wearing a works uniform or was hurrying to work they would make sure that everyone nearby would hear it, and, most importantly, all respond accordingly.

The phrase was about respect, about solidarity, about demonstrating basic decency to someone else no matter what they were doing, and to over the invisibilisation of so many people's labour. No one's labours were dismissed as low status or menial, everyone was a comrade, someone who would be your ally in any attempt to bring about meaningful change in society. It was about seeing beyond the divisions and fragmentations of neoliberal capitalist realism. Making way for the worker is a form of Honneth's recognition theory. The intersubjectivity of social agents is emphasized and, crucially, another subject is 'recognised as a person whose capabilities are of constitutive value to a concrete community' (Honneth and Farrell 1997: 20).

Some forms of work are affected by an occupational stigma. In the classic formulation of this concept by Ashford and Kreiner (1999), this applies to dirty work, where the worker comes into contact with physical dirt, stigmatized groups or the work itself sits outside moral norms. Earlier explorations of this concept focused on sanitation workers, service workers and sex workers. More recently, research in this area has extended occupational stigma to areas such as hospitality and other work that is low-paid, or low in status. As with all stigmas it exerts an effect on the wellbeing of the stigma recipient. As Kusluvan et al (2022) have noted in their research, occupational stigma leads to low self-worth and self-esteem. At worst, it can lead to the dehumanization of low-paid, low-status workers (Volapto et al 2017), while Benach et al (2014) have speculated that precarious employment may need to be considered a further social determinant of health.

The treatment of low-paid, low-status workers can be read as a form of alienation, as Volpato et al (2017) have argued. It is other-person alienation where the value and worth of another worker ceases to be recognized and they are perceived as an object, devoid of any qualities that should grant them intersubjective recognition. As increasing amounts of work is low-status, which carries with it the risks of becoming alienated from other workers, and the consequences that will have for wellbeing, then making way for all workers and granting recognition of worth and equal status is a step against alienation and the beginnings of moving against the worst alienating, fragmenting and atomizing tendencies within neoliberal capitalism. It is not a grand revolutionary activity but a small step in a wider process that helps to care for others (and for yourself). Here's another small step and then an idea that stretches out from the everyday.

Juking the stats, juking the algorithm and juking alienation

The invisible hand of neoliberalism appears in every episode of *The Wire*, first broadcast in the early 2000s. Beneath the grit and grime of urban deprivation circulations of money flow through every episode, everything is commodified or measured. Investigating the apartment of arch-criminal Stringer Bell (played by Idris Elba) the police come across a copy of Adam Smith's *Wealth of Nations* on his shelf. It was part of his reading to legitimate his drug dealing and money laundering, but acting as a metaphor for how everything, including what is deemed to be illegal, fits with the logics of capital. The show probably feels dated now, but in its heyday, it revealed how the essential shallowness of everyday neoliberal technologies made situations worse or could easily be undone and in some ways be resisted.

Juking the stats was one mode of resistance or adaptation to the quantification or metrification of everyday life.

In his redemptive arc former policeman Prez (Pryzbylewski) begins a new career in teaching. On his first day he and his colleagues are instructed by school management at a staff meeting that their ratings and outcomes need to improve. The announcement is met with consternation and disbelief. On first impression it appears they will have to do much more work in impossibly tight timeframes. But he realizes what to do, they just need to juke the stats and what they have been told to do can be easily and painlessly subverted. 'Juke the stats and majors become colonels', he says about the charade of statistics as he informs a colleague how they can subvert the school policy. All they have to do is to meet a statistical threshold, nothing actually has to change on the ground. No arrests have to be made, all that is required is that a number has to be entered that indicate arrests have to be made. That is the measure and therefore that is all that has to be done. From then on it is heads down, take it easy and relax. Just juke the stats and all is fine. The measure is everything.

Contemporary lives are saturated with invitations to complete feedback on how other human beings have acted in circumstances not of their own choosing, following a labour process they had no control over and ultimately as part of a commodifying nexus that also includes the customer, who is objectively another worker. The disciplinary function of ratings works in two directions. It is just not the worker that is disciplined. The ratings system functions to monitor and thereby deepen the exploitation of workers, the managerial gaze constantly pursuing the worker. But ratings also discipline the other social agent in this process of quality control. They are brought into the neoliberal discourse of assessment and new management, becoming part of the enactment of capitalist power. This is other person alienation. The customer becomes part of the control apparatus of the labour process, they in that moment set themselves apart from the other person, and ally, unwittingly so, with the exploitation of that person and their objectification.

Anker makes the following very valid objection to juking the stats:

> Juking the stats, for one, does not necessarily construct more humane, democratic institutions. Nor does it generate more support for students or the vulnerable, or re-shape society toward economic and racial equality. It is reactionary, in that it reacts against neoliberal imperatives but is seemingly bereft of a motivating vision for the future other than countering the present. (Anker 2016: 769)

As depicted in *The Wire*, it was reactive, but juking does not have to be like that. The form of juking advocated here is about recognizing the relationship between the activities of another human and yourself. It is about understanding how capitalist power functions and flows on a daily basis.

It may not seem that revolutionary, but it is about poking holes in the capitalist realism, about steeping aside from everyday enactments of alienation, and rendering obsolete a contemporary form of managerial control over the labour process. So, give every worker five stars out of five for their performance, fill in every evaluation form that everything was perfect and see rating schemes for what they are: a form of control over yourself and other people.

Join a trade union

The previous forms of solidarity were in everyday life, about breaking down the individualization and fragmentation of how we relate to ourselves and to others. They have their role in preventing all aspects of existence becoming subsumed into the logics of neoliberal capitalism. But that is only a beginning. Trade unionism is a form of collective solidarity that stretches out beyond a specific and passing point of time. It is about each working for all and standing by others to raise working conditions and to act as a counterweight to the power of capital.

As the work of Muntaner and colleagues has indicated, trade unionism is good for health and wealth. Countries with high levels of trade union membership and trade union strength tend to be healthier and express higher levels of wellbeing across a number of areas. The historical formation of trade unions in Brazil, for example, assisted in improving the overall wellbeing of workers there (Renwick 2009). Blanchflower and Bryson (2020: 6), drawing more recently on the data from nearly two million respondents in the United States, found that '[o]n many dimensions, relating to work, wellbeing, time trust and macro issues union members are more satisfied than non-members'.

Trade unions provide a major bulwark against capitalism operating freely and unfettered over the labour process. Trade unions have been critical to winning either major concessions from exploitation or protecting what workers have gained in previous struggles. Challenges do exist for trade unions operating within neoliberalism. Grady (2013) had pointed to how trade unions must walk a fine line between accommodating to neoliberalism and confronting its assault on workers and their conditions. Neoliberalism, Grady maintains, has created a discourse that, without a viable left alternative, sets the parameters of what is feasible – another instance of capitalist realism. That aside, unions are one source in society that can countervail the tendencies within capitalism for alienation. They do so by providing a counterbalance to the asymmetrical power imbalances within the work with their connections to (supposedly) progressive political parties but also through the mobilization of working-class power in the form of labour disputes.

One other way that unions could counter alienation and promote better wellbeing in the workplace and in the wider community is campaigning for increased economic democracy within society (Yuill 2010). Economic democracy takes many forms, but the central tenet is some form of diffusion of power within an organization away from management out to the workforce, creating multiple rather than one locus of power. Control over the labour process can be opened up to the desires and needs of the workforce, and therefore act as a countervailing tendency to alienation.

Economic democracy is though still a form of capitalism, leaving the core relation of worker and capital, and the relation with the market intact, but it does advance the idea that the current status quo of hyper-managerialism with every aspect of the labour process being subjected to ever more levels of micro-surveillance is not the only form that work can take. I do not therefore envisage economic democracy as an end in itself which would instantly solve the problems inherent in capitalist modes of production. It is rather a transitional form, something that could lead to a post-capitalist society, and in doing so begin to deal with the negative experiences of working within capitalist realism at the present rather than postponing everything to a desired future that could be some way off.

Economic democracy can be in the form of shares, it can be in the form of teamwork, or it can be much more radical. As I have discussed elsewhere (Yuill 2010), the share option and increased teamworking options may seem superficially attractive, with an outward gloss of workers having some form of technical or symbolic control. But they do not have what for me is vital in any form of economic democracy, which is control and influence over the labour process. For example, Baldry et al (1998) have critiqued teamworking as a form of Team Taylorism, where the workers themselves become responsible for their own exploitation.

Final thoughts

I am writing this when the world appears to be in flux and turmoil. In some accelerationist imaginaries the collapse of so many taken-for-granted norms that have existed since the fall of the Berlin Wall would be welcome. The opportunities for change always appear to increase the more a society begins to fall apart, and new possibilities for change emerge. The main beneficiaries of the current chaos, however, seem to be of the right, if not the *far* right. While the populism of Trump appears to have been checked in America by the Biden presidency, his distinctive version of American Nativism remains a powerful force in American society. Trump may disappear in a welter of lawsuits, but he could be a vanishing mediator, in a permanent shift in the

United States to a less democratic and authoritarian society. It seems at the moment it is the morbid symptoms that appear when society is in flux that are gaining the upper hand.

Jameson's much quoted (and frequently mis-attributed to Žižek) observation that it is easier to imagine the end of the world than the end of capitalism gains greater prescience. In addition to wars and ongoing conflict, not just in Ukraine but also in places like Yemen, long-term and destructive environmental change is occurring. At the time of writing, 30 million have been affected by flooding in Pakistan, considerably more than the seven million displaced in Ukraine by the war.

The world is still emerging from the COVID-19 pandemic,[4] a singular historical event that challenged so many fundamentals of society, on multiple scales. Reflecting on epidemics, the insightful medical sociology essayist Phil Strong wrote about what he called 'epidemic psychology'. He was writing at the time of the AIDS epidemic in the 1980s, and drew into his analysis both what was occurring then and lessons from other plagues, the Black Death in particular. One lesson is that microscopic viruses possess a powerful agency that can exert fundamental social changes, which interact with other economic and social relations producing some form of social change. At some points in the COVID-19 pandemic a small glimpse appeared of a world less dense in consumerism, with novel approaches to work and glimmers of a new wider and deeper solidarity (for more on this observation see Yuill 2021). Whether these embers of change can become something greater waits to be seen. One trend in workplaces of the Global North is quiet quitting – a variant of Fleming and Sewell's (2002) '*švejkism*' discussed earlier. Quiet quitting is nothing to do with leaving your job. Prompted by the COVID-19 pandemic,[5] some workers have taken stock of their lives and decided that work is not everything and re-evaluated their lives. The upshot of which is to do the least possible at work, to not go beyond the bare minimum of an employer's expectation to create as much time as they can for their own pursuits. On one level that is welcome as it means a beginning of a break with capitalist realism, but it is hardly the rush and push of a deep transformation.

It is perhaps in the Global South that resistance to neoliberalism, colonialism and capitalism is most obviously apparent. Movements such as the

---

[4] In fact, as Hamlin (2009) notes in his work on Cholera, the regularity of pandemics and epidemics in history is perhaps an omission in Marx's analysis in the dynamics of history. That is a point worth returning to at some other juncture.

[5] There has also been talk of the Great Resignation where workers were supposedly quitting their jobs en masse and either looking for work they deemed more rewarding or exiting the labour force entirely. I agree with Krugman's (2022) analysis that this trend may be illusory and something of an urban legend. There appears to be a lack of supporting evidence.

Zapatistas in the Chiapas region of Mexico are the obvious examples. Their struggles have led to the creation of autonomous zones that offer alternative models of social organization and cooperation. It is vital that if alienation has to be overcome then it requires change on a global scale, change in the global north is insufficient. Alienation emerges from deep structures that run through global history woven out of the rise of capitalism and the spread of colonialism and any solution to alienation has to understand that history.

Then again, the prospects for deeper and more fundamental change or for some form of radical action always seem bleak and distant. French Marxist Andre Gorz (1967) famously predicted that we should forget a proletarian revolution. Within a few months he was proven wrong by the 1968 uprisings. When change comes it will be a combination of human agency and structural crisis, but in what direction that will be is another question.

And to that end: the future is unwritten.

References

Aiken, M. and Hage, J. (1966) 'Organizational Alienation: A Comparative Analysis', *American Sociological Review* 31(4): 497–507.

Althusser, L. (1969) *For Marx*. London: Allen Lane.

Althusser, L. (2005) *For Marx*. London: Verso.

Anderson, B.R.O. (2016) *Imagined Communities*. London: Verso.

Anderson, K.B. (2016) *Marx at the Margins*. Chicago: University of Chicago Press.

Anker, E.R. (2016) 'Thwarting Neoliberal Security: Ineptitude, the Retrograde, and the Uninspiring in "The Wire"', *American Literary History*, 28(4): 759–778.

Archibald, W.P. (1978) 'Using Marx's Theory of Alienation Empirically', *Theory and Society* 6(1): 119–132.

Arditi, B. (2006) 'Louis Althusser'. In T. Carver (ed) *Palgrave Advances in Continental Political Thought*. Basingstoke: Palgrave, pp 182–195.

Aristotle (2004) *The Nicomachean Ethics*. London: Penguin Classics.

Ashforth, B.E. and Kreiner, G.E. (1999) '"How can you do it?": Dirty Work and the Challenge of Constructing a Positive Identity', *Academy of Management Review* 24(3): 413–434.

Averini, S. (1996) 'Labor, Alienation and Social Classes in Hegel's *Realphilosophie*', in J. O'Neil (ed) *Hegel's Dialectic of Desire and Recognition*. Albany: State of New York University Press, pp 96–119.

Bachelard, G. (1968) *The Philosophy of No: A Philosophy of the New Scientific Mind*. New York: Orion Press.

Baldry, C., Bain, P. and Taylor, P. (1998) ' "Bright Satanic Offices": Intensification, Control and Team Taylorism', in P. Thompson and C. Warhurst (eds) *Workplaces of the Future*. London: Macmillan Education UK, pp 163–183.

Barakat, H. (1969) 'Alienation: A Process of Encounter Between Utopia and Reality', *British Journal of Sociology* 20(1): 1–10.

Bastani, A. (2019) *Fully Automated Luxury Communism: A Manifesto*. London: Verso.

Bauman, Z. (1998) *Work, Consumerism and the New Poor*. Philadelphia: Open University Press.

Benach, J., Vives, A., Amable, M., Vanroelen, C., Tarafa, G. and Muntaner, C. (2014) 'Precarious Employment: Understanding an Emerging Social Determinant of Health', *Annual Review of Public Health* 35(1): 229–253.

Bendelow, G.A. and Williams, S.J. (2002) *The Lived Body: Sociological Themes, Embodied Issues.* London: Routledge.

Bennett, J. (2010) *Vibrant Matter.* Durham: Duke University Press.

Bensaïd, D. (2009) *A Marx for Our Times: Adventures and Misadventures of a Critique.* New York: Verso.

Benton, T. (1991) 'Biology and Social Science: Why the Return of the Repressed Should Be Given a (Cautious) Welcome', *Sociology* 25(1): 1–29.

Benton, T. (1993) *Natural Relations: Ecology, Animal Rights and Social Justice.* New York: Verso.

Berggren, Henrik and Trägårdh, Lars (2011) 'Social Trust and Radical Individualism: The Paradox at the Heart of Nordic Capitalism', *The Nordic Way*: 13–22.

Berman, M. (1999) *Adventures in Marxism.* New York: Verso.

Betti, E. (2016) 'Gender and Precarious Labor in a Historical Perspective: Italian Women and Precarious Work Between Fordism and Post-Fordism', *International Labor and Working-Class History* 89: 64–83.

Bhaskar, R. (1975) *A Realist Theory of Science.* Leeds: Leeds Books.

Billig, M. (2013) *Learn to Write Badly.* West Nyack: Cambridge University Press.

Blackburn, R.M. and Mann, M.M. (1979) *The Working Class in the Labour Market.* London: Macmillan.

Blackledge, P. (2012) *Marxism and Ethics: Freedom, Desire, and Revolution.* New York: State University of New York Press.

Blanchflower, D.G. and Bryson, A. (2020) 'Now Unions Increase Job Satisfaction and Well-being' (No. w27720). National Bureau of Economic Research.

Blauner, R. (1964) *Alienation and Freedom: The Factory Worker and His Industry.* Chicago: University of Chicago Press.

Bosma, H., Marmot, M.G., Hemingway, H., Nicholson, A.C., Brunner, E. and Stansfield, S.A. (1997) 'Low Job Control and Risk of Coronary Heart Disease in Whitehall II (Prospective Cohort) Study', *British Medical Journal* 314(7080): 558–565.

Braverman, H. (1998) *Labor and Monopoly Capital: The Degradation of Work in the Twentieth Century.* New York: Monthly Review Press.

Brenner, N. (1994) 'Foucault's New Functionalism', *Theory and Society* 23(5): 679–709.

Brenner, N., Peck, J. and Theodore, N. (2010) 'Variegated Neoliberalization: Geographies, Modalities, Pathways', *Global Networks* 10(2): 182–222.

Brewer, J.D. (1989) 'Conjectural History, Sociology and Social Change in Eighteenth-Century Scotland: Adam Ferguson and the Division of Labor', in D. McCrone, S. Kendrick and P. Straw (eds) *The Making of Scotland: Nation, Culture and Social Change*. Edinburgh: Edinburgh University Press, pp 13–30.

Brewer, J.D. (2007) 'Putting Adam Ferguson in His Place', *The British Journal of Sociology* 58(1): 105–122.

Brunner, E. (2009) 'Health Inequalities and the Role of Psychosocial Work Factors: The Whitehall II Study', in S.J. Babones (ed) *Social Inequality and Public Health*. Bristol: Policy Press, pp 114–130.

Burawoy, M. (1998) 'The Extended Case Method', *Sociological Theory* 16(1): 4–33.

Byron, C. (2013) 'The Normative Force behind Marx's Theory of Alienation', *Critique* 41(3): 427–435.

Cacioppo, J.T. and Cacioppo, S. (2014) 'Social Relationships and Health: The Toxic Effects of Perceived Social Isolation', *Social and Personality Psychology Compass* 8(2): 58–72.

Cacioppo, J.T. and Patrick, W. (2008) *Loneliness: Human Nature and the Need for Human Connection*. New York: Norton.

Callinicos, A. (1976) *Althusser's Marxism*. London: Pluto Press.

Callinicos, A. (1982) *Is there a Future for Marxism?* London: Palgrave Macmillan.

Callinicos, A. (1989) 'Anthony Giddens: A Contemporary Critique', in A. Callinicos (ed) *Marxist Theory*. Oxford: Oxford University Press.

Callinicos, A. (1999) *Social Theory: A Historical Introduction*. Cambridge: Polity.

Calnan, M. and Wainwright, D. (2002) *Work Stress: The Making of a Modern Epidemic*. Buckingham: Open University Press.

Carey, M. (2008) 'Everything Must Go? The Privatisation of State Social Work', *British Journal of Social Work* 38(5): 918–935.

Carlisle, S., Henderson, G. and Hanlon, P.W. (2009) '"Wellbeing": A Collateral Casualty of Modernity?', *Social Science and Medicine* 69(10): 1556–1560.

Carlyle, T. (1829) *Sign of the Times*. Kindle Download.

Carpenter, A.N. (2010) 'The Aristotelian Heart of Marx's Condemnation of Capitalism', *Studia Philosophica Wratislaviensia* 5(4): 41–64.

Carter, C.S. (2017) 'The Role of Oxytocin and Vasopressin in Attachment', *Psychodynamic Psychiatry* 45(4): 499–517.

Carver, T. (2008) 'Marx's Conception of Alienation in the Grundrisse'. In M. Musto (ed) *Karl Marx's Grundrisse: Foundations of the Critique of Political Economy 150 Years Later*. Abingdon: Routledge, pp 48–66.

Casarino, C. (2011) 'Marx before Spinoza: Notes toward an Investigation'. In D. Vardoulakis (ed) *Spinoza Now*. Minneapolis: University of Minnesota Press, pp 179–34.

Case, A. and Deaton, A. (2020) *Deaths of Despair and the Future of Capitalism*. Princeton: Princeton University Press.

CDC (Centers for Disease Control and Prevention) (2022) 'Understanding the Opioid Overdose Epidemic'. https://www.cdc.gov/opioids/basics/epidemic.html

Christie, N.C. (2021) 'The Role of Social Isolation in Opioid Addiction', *Social Cognitive and Affective Neuroscience* 16(7): 645–656.

Clark, A.E. and Oswald, A.J. (1994) 'Unhappiness and Unemployment', *The Economic Journal* 104(424): 648–659.

Clark, A.E. and Oswald, A.J. (1996) 'Satisfaction and Comparison Income', *Journal of Public Economics* 61(3): 359–381.

Clark, J.P. (1959) 'Measuring Alienation within a Social System', *American Sociological Review* 24(6): 849–852.

Coburn, D. (1979) 'Job Alienation and Well-Being', *International Journal of Health Services* 9(1): 41–59.

Cockerham, W.C. (2007) 'A Note on the Fate of Postmodern Theory and Its Failure to Meet the Basic Requirements for Success in Medical Sociology', *Social Theory and Health* 5(4): 285–296.

Coelho, H.F., Canter, P.H. and Ernst, E. (2013) 'Mindfulness-Based Cognitive Therapy: Evaluating Current Evidence and Informing Future Research', *Journal of Consulting and Clinical Psychology* 75(6): 1000–1005.

Cohen, G.A. (2001) *Karl Marx's Theory of History: A Defence*. Princeton: Princeton University Press.

Corrigan, P. and Leonard, P. (1978) *Social Work and Capitalism*. London: Macmillan.

Coryn, C.L.S., Noakes, L.A., Westine, C.D. and Schroter, D.C. (2010) 'A Systematic Review of Theory-driven Evaluation Practice from 1990–2009', *American Journal of Evaluation* 32(20): 199–226.

Cowie, J. (2012) *Stayin' Alive: The 1970s and the Last Days of the Working Class*. New York: The New Press.

Cowling, M. (2006) Alienation in the Older Marx. *Contemporary Political Theory* 5: 319–339.

Cox, J. (1998) 'An Introduction to Marx's Theory of Alienation', *International Socialism* 2(79): 41–62.

Creaven, S. (2000) *Marxism and Realism: A Materialist Application of Realism in the Social Sciences*. London: Routledge.

Crinson, I. and Yuill, C. (2008) 'What Alienation Theory can Contribute to the Study of Health Inequalities', *International Journal of Health Service* 38(3): 455–470.

Cronin de Chavez, A., Backett-Milburn, K., Parry, O. and Platt, S. (2005) 'Understanding and Researching Wellbeing: Its Usage in Different Disciplines and Potential for Health Promotion', *Health Education Journal* 64(1): 70–87.

Csikszentmihalyi, M. (1990) *Flow: The Psychology of Optimal Experience*. New York: Harper & Row.

Csikszentmihalyi, M. (1997) *Finding Flow*. New York: Basic.

Damasio, A. (2005) *Descartes' Error: Emotion, Reason, and the Human Brain*. London: Penguin.

Danermark, B., Ekström, M., Jakobsen L. and Karlsson, J.C. (2002) *Explaining Society*. London: Routledge.

Dardot, P. and Laval, C. (2013) *The New Way of the World: On Neoliberal Society*. London: Verso.

De Dreu, C.K. (2012) 'Oxytocin Modulates Cooperation within and Competition Between Groups: An Integrative Review and Research Agenda', *Hormones and Behavior* 61(3): 419–428.

De Dreu, C.K. and Kret, M.E. (2016) 'Oxytocin Conditions Intergroup Relations through Unregulated In-group Empathy, Cooperation, Conformity, and Defense', *Biological Psychiatry* 79(3): 165–173.

Deci, E.L. and Ryan, R.M. (2008) 'Hedonia, Eudaimonia: An Introduction', *Journal of Happiness Studies* 9: 1–11.

Deleuze, G. (1992) 'Postscript on the Societies of Control', *October* 59: 3–7.

Della Volpe, G. (1980) *Logic as a Positive Science*. London: Verso.

Dickens, P. (2002) *Reconstructing Nature: Alienation, Emancipation and the Division of Labour*. London: Routledge.

Duggan, L. (2019) *Mean Girl: Ayn Rand and the Culture of Greed*. Berkeley: University of California Press.

Duhe, A (2017) 'The Concept of Indignation in Spinozist Marxism', *Historical Materialism*. https://www.historicalmaterialism.org/blog/conc ept-indignation-spinozist-marxism

Duncan, J. (2021) *Take it Easy Island: Portland in the 1970s*. Yarmouth: Islandport Press.

Dyer-Witheford, N. (2004) '1844/2004/2044: The Return of Species-Being', *Historical Materialism: Research in Critical Marxist Theory* 12(4): 1–23.

Dyer-Witheford, N. (2009) 'Twenty-First Century Species-Being', Sixth Annual Marx and Philosophy Conference, Institute of Education, University of London.

Eakin, J. and MacEachen, E. (1998) 'Health and the Social Relations of Work: A Study of the Health-related Experiences of Employees in Small Workplaces', *Sociology of Health and Illness* 20(6): 896–914.

Eastwood, M.J., Frischen, A., Fenske, M.J. and Smilek, D. (2012) 'The Unengaged Mind: Defining Boredom in Terms of Attention', *Perspectives on Psychological Science* 7(5): 482–495.

Eco, U. (1983) 'Horns, Hooves, Insteps', in U. Eco and T.A. Sebeok (eds) *The Sign of Three, Dupin, Holmes, Peirce*. Bloomington: Indiana University Press, pp 199–219.

Elias, N. (2000) *The Civilizing Process*. Malden: Blackwell Publishing.

Elliott, G. (1987) *Althusser: The Detour of Theory*. London: Verso.

Elster, J. (1985) *Making Sense of Marx*. Cambridge: Cambridge University Press.

Engels, F. (1975) *The Part Played by Labour in the Transition from Ape to Man*. Beijing: Foreign Languages Press.

Engels, F. (1993) *The Condition of the Working Class in England*. Oxford: Oxford University Press.

Engels, F. (2015) *Socialism, Utopian and Scientific*. CreateSpace Independent Publishing Platform.

Evans, T. (2010) *Professional Discretion in Welfare Services*. London: Ashgate.

Fahlgren, S. (2009) 'Discourse Analysis of a Childcare Drama: Or the Interfaces Between Paradoxical Discourses of Time in the Context of Social Work', *Time & Society* 18(2–3): 208–230.

Falótico, T., Proffitt, T., Ottoni, E.B., Staff, R.A. and Haslam, M. (2019) 'Three Thousand Years of Wild Capuchin Stone Tool Use', *Nature Ecology & Evolution* 3(7): 1034–1038.

Fana, M. (2016) 'Frédéric Lordon: "Put an end to the empire of capital"', *Il Manifesto*. https://global.ilmanifesto.it/frederic-lordon-put-an-end-to-the-empire-of-capital/

Fanon, F. (2001) *The Wretched of the Earth*. London: Penguin.

Fanon, F. (2021a) *Black Skin, White Masks*. London: Penguin.

Fanon, F (2021b) *The Psychiatric Writings from Alienation and Freedom*. London: Bloomsbury Academic.

Ferguson, I. (2008) *Reclaiming Social Work: Challenging Neo-liberalism and Promoting Social Justice*. London: SAGE.

Ferguson, I. and Lavalette, M. (2004) 'Beyond Power Discourse: Alienation and Social Work', *British Journal of Social Work* 34(3): 297–312.

Filip, B. (2012) 'Polanyi and Hayek on Freedom, the State, and Economics', *International Journal of Political Economy* 41(4): 69–87.

Fisher, M. (2009) *Capitalist Realism*. London: Zero Books.

Fisher, M. (2014) *Ghosts of My Life: Writings on Depression, Hauntology and Lost Futures*. Winchester: Zero Books.

Fisher, M. (2017) *The Weird and the Eerie*. London: Repeater Book.

Fisher M. (2018) *K-punk: The Collected and Unpublished Writings of Mark Fisher (2004–2016)*. London: Repeater Books.

Fisher, M. (2020) *Postcapitalist Desire: The Final Lectures*. London: Repeater Books.

Fisher, M. (2022) 'Acid Communism', *Purple Magazine* 37. https://purple.fr/magazine/the-future-issue-37-s-s-2022/acid-communism/

Fleetwood, S. (2012) Laws and Tendencies in Marxist Political Economy. *Capital & Class* 36(2): 235–262.

Fleming, P. (2015) *The Mythology of Work: How Capitalism Persists Despite Itself*. London: Pluto Press.

Fleming, P. and Sewell, G. (2002) 'Looking for the Good Soldier, Švejk: Alternative Modalities of Resistance in the Contemporary Workplace', *Sociology* 36(4): 857–873.

Fleming, P., Roberts, J. and Garsten, C. (2013) 'In Search of Corporate Social Responsibility: Introduction to Special Issue', *Organization* 20(3): 337–348.

Forbes, A. and Wainwright, S.P. (2001) 'On the Methodological, Theoretical and Philosophical Context of Health Inequalities Research: A Critique', *Social Science & Medicine* 53(6): 801–816.

Foster, J.B. (2000) *Marx's Ecology: Materialism and Nature*. New York: Monthly Review Press.

Foster, J.B. and Clark, B. (2016) 'Marx's Ecology and the Left', *Monthly Review* 68(2): 1–25.

Foucault, M. (1990) *The Care of the Self: The History of Sexuality Vol. 3*. London: Penguin.

Foucault, M. (1997) *Ethics: Subjectivity and Truth*. New York: The New Press.

Foucault, M. (1998a) *The Will to Knowledge: The History of Sexuality Vol. 1*. London: Penguin.

Foucault, M. (1998b) *The Use of Pleasure: The History of Sexuality Vol. 2*. London: Penguin.

Foucault, M. (2002) *The Birth of the Clinic*. London: Routledge.

Fox, N.J. and Alldred, P. (2016) *Sociology and the New Materialism*. London: Sage.

Fracchia, J. (2005) 'Beyond the Human–Nature Debate: Human Corporeal Organisation as the "First Fact" of Historical Materialism'. *Historical Materialism* 13(1): 33–36.

Freeman, J.B. (2001) *Working-Class New York: Life and Labor Since World War II*. New York: New Press.

Fromm, E. (1979) *To Have or To Be?* London: Abacus.

Fromm, E. (2002) *The Sane Society*. London: Routledge.

Geras, N. (1985) *Marx and Human Nature: Refutation of a Legend*. London: Verso.

Gerhardt, U. (1989) *Ideas about Illness: An Intellectual and Political History of Medical Sociology*. New York: New York University Press.

Giddens, A. (1998) *The Third Way: The Renewal of Social Democracy*. Cambridge: Polity Press.

Goleman, D. (1996) *Emotional Intelligence: Why it Can Matter More Than IQ*. London: Bloomsbury.

Gorz, A. (1967) *La Socialisme Difficile*. Paris: Editions du Seuil.

Grady, J. (2013) 'Trade Unions and the Pension Crisis: Defending Member Interests in a Neoliberal World', *Employee Relations*, 35(3): 294–308.

Graeber, D. (2018) *Bullshit Jobs*. New York: Simon & Schuster.

Graeber, D. and Wengrow, D. (2021) *The Dawn of Everything: A New History of Humanity*. London: Penguin.

Gray, D. (2009) *Homage to Caledonia: Scotland and the Spanish Civil War.* Edinburgh: Luath.

Greaves, M.D. (2016) 'Cycles of Alienation: Technology and Control in Digital Communication', *New Proposals: Journal of Marxism and Interdisciplinary Inquiry* 9(1): 49–63.

Habermas, J. (1978) *Knowledge and Human Interests.* London: Heinemann Educational.

Habermas, J. (1990) *The Philosophical Discourse of Modernity: Twelve Lectures.* Cambridge, MA: MIT Press.

Hall, S. (2003) 'Marx's Notes on Method: A "Reading" of the "1857 Introduction"', *Cultural Studies* 17(2): 113–149.

Hall, S., Critcher, C., Jefferson, T., Clarke, J. and Roberts, B. (1978) *Policing the Crisis: Mugging, the State and Law and Order.* London: Macmillan.

Hamlin, C. (2009) *Cholera: The Biography.* Oxford: Oxford University Press.

Hardt, M. and Negri, A. (2000) *Empire.* Cambridge: Harvard University Press.

Hardt, M. and Negri, A. (2005) *Multitude: War and Democracy in the Age of Empire.* London: Penguin.

Hardt, M. and Negri, A. (2009) *Commonwealth.* Cambridge: Harvard University Press.

Harman, C. (2009) *Zombie Capitalism: Global Crisis and the Relevance of Marx.* London: Bookmarks.

Harris, J. (1998) 'Scientific Management, Bureau-Professionalism and New Managerialism: The Labour Process of State Social Work', *The British Journal of Social Work* 28(6): 839–862.

Harris, J. (2003) *The Social Work Business.* London: Routledge.

Harvey, D. (2007) *A Brief History of Neoliberalism.* Oxford: Oxford University Press.

Harvey, D. (2018) 'Universal Alienation', *Journal for Cultural Research* 22(2): 137–150.

Hatton, E. (2015) 'Work beyond the Bounds: A Boundary Analysis of the Fragmentation of Work', *Work, Employment and Society* 29(6): 1007–1018.

Hatton, E. (2017) 'Mechanisms of Invisibility: Rethinking the Concept of Invisible Work', *Work, Employment and Society* 31(2): 336–351.

Haworth, J. and Hart, G. (2012) *Well-being: Individual, Community and Social Perspectives.* Houndmills: Palgrave Macmillan.

Hill, L. (2007) 'Adam Smith, Adam Ferguson and Karl Marx on the Division of Labor', *Journal of Classical Sociology* 7(3): 339–366.

Hindess, B. and Hirst, P.Q. (1975) *Pre-Capitalist Modes of Production.* London: Routledge & Kegan Paul.

Hirst, P.Q. (1976) 'Althusser and the Theory of Ideology', *Economy and Society* 5(4): 385–412.

Ho, K. (2009) *Liquidated: An Ethnography of Wall Street.* Durham, NC: Duke University Press.

Hochschild, A. (1983) *The Managed Heart: Commercialization of Human Feeling*. Berkley: University of California Press.

Honneth, A. and Farrell, J. (1997) 'Recognition and Moral Obligation', *Social Research*: 16–35.

Horrocks, C. and Johnson, S. (2014) 'Developing a Relational and Socially Situated Approach to Informing Action to Improve Health and Well-being', *Sociology of Health and Illness* 36(2): 175–186.

Howson, A. and Inglis, D. (2001) 'The Body in Sociology: Tensions Inside and Outside Sociological Thought', *The Sociological Review* 49(3): 297–317.

Hughes, J. (2003) ' "Intelligent Hearts": Emotional Intelligence, Emotional Labour and Informalization', *CLMS Working Paper No 43*. Leicester: University of Leicester.

Huppert, F.A. (2014) 'The State of Well-being Science: Concepts, Measures, Interventions and Policies', in F.A. Huppert and C.L. Cooper (eds) *Interventions and Policies to Enhance Well-being*. London: Wiley Blackwell, pp 1–49.

Jaeggi, R. (2014) *Alienation*. New York: Columbia University Press.

Jaffe, S. (2021) *Work Won't Love You Back: How Devotion to Our Jobs Keeps Us Exploited, Exhausted, and Alone*. New York: Bold Type Books.

Jakubowski, F. (1990) *Ideology and Superstructure in Historical Materialism* (trans. A. Booth). London: Pluto.

Jameson, F. (2010) *Representing Capital: A Reading of Volume One*. London: Verso.

Jensen, K.B. (1995) *The Social Semiotics of Mass Communication*. London: SAGE.

Jones, C. (2001) 'Voices from the Front Line: State Social Workers and New Labour', *British Journal of Social Work* 31(4): 547–562.

Kahneman, D., Diner, E. and Schwarz, N. (1999) *Well-being: The Foundations of Hedonic Psychology*. New York: The Russell Sage Foundation.

Kanungo, R.N. (1983) 'Work Alienation: A Pancultural Perspective', *International Studies of Management & Organization* 13(1–2): 119–138.

Kanungo, R.N. (1990) 'Culture and Work Alienation Western Models and Eastern Realities', *International Journal of Psychology* 25(3–6): 795–812.

Keltner, D. (2009) *Born to Be Good: The Science of a Meaningful Life*. New York: W.W. Norton & Company.

Krieger, N. (2020) 'Measures of Racism, Sexism, Heterosexism, and Gender Binarism for Health Equity Research: From Structural Injustice to Embodied Harm – An Ecosocial Analysis', *Annual Review of Public Health* 41(1): 37–62.

Krugman, P. (2022) 'What Ever Happened to the Great Resignation?', *New York Times*, 5 April.

Kusluvan, H., Akova, O. and Kusluvan, S. (2022) 'Occupational Stigma and Career Commitment: Testing Mediation and Moderation Effects of Occupational Self-esteem', *International Journal of Hospitality Management* 102(10): 103149.

Labriola, A. (2005) *Essays on the Materialistic Conception of History*. New York: Cosmio Classics.

Lachowycz, K. and Jones, A.P. (2014) 'Does Walking Explain Associations Between Access to Greenspace and Lower Mortality?' *Social Science & Medicine* 107: 9–17.

Lakatos, I. (1980) *Methodology of Scientific Research Programmes: Philosophical Papers: v. 1*. Cambridge: Cambridge University Press.

Lavalette, M. and Ferguson, I. (2018) 'Marx: Alienation, Commodity Fetishism and the World of Contemporary Social Work', *Critical and Radical Social Work* 6(2): 197–213.

Lazzarato, M. (1996) 'Immaterial Labour', in M. Hardt and P. Virno (eds) Radical *Thought in Italy: A Potential Politics*, Minneapolis and London: University of Minnesota Press, pp 133–147.

Lebowitz, M. (2003) *Beyond Capital*. Houndmills: Palgrave.

Leder, D. (2012) 'Old McDonald's had a Farm: The Metaphysics of Factory Farming', *Journal of Animal Ethics* 2(1): 73–86.

Lefebvre, H. (1968) *Dialectical Materialism*. London: Cape.

Lefebvre, H. (2004) *Rhythmanalysis: Space, Time and Everyday Life*. London: Continuum.

Lefebvre, L. (2014) *Critique of Everyday Life: The One Volume Edition*. London: Verso.

Levine, N. (2021) *Marx's Resurrection of Aristotle*. Cham: Springer Nature.

Levins, R. (2007) *Biology under the Influence: Dialectical Essays on the Coevolution of Nature and Society*. New York: New York University Press.

Levins, R. and Lewontin, R.C. (1985) *The Dialectic Biologist*. Cambridge, MA: Harvard University Press.

Lewis, J. (1972) 'The Althusser Case', *Marxism Today*, January: 23–28 and February: 43–48.

Lewontin, R. (2007) *The Triple Helix: Gene, Organism, and Environment*. Cambridge, MA: Harvard University Press.

Linebaugh, P. (2003) *The London Hanged: Crime and Civil Society in the Eighteenth Century* (2nd edition). New York: Verso.

Little, D. (2011) 'Marxism and Method', *Understanding Society*. http://www-personal.umd.umich.edu/~delittle/Marxism%20and%20Method%203.htm

Liu, T. and Csikszentmihalyi, M. (2020) 'Flow among Introverts and Extraverts in Solitary and Social Activities', *Personality and Individual Differences* 167: 110197.

Lordon, F. (2014) *Willing Slaves of Capital: Spinoza and Marx on Desire*. New York: Verso.

Lordon, F. (2022) *Imperium*. New York: Verso.

Lukács, G. (1975) *History and Class Consciousness: Studies in Marxist Dialectics*. London: Merlin.

MacCannell, D. (1976) *The Tourist: A New Theory of the Leisure Class.* New York: Schocken.

Magnani, L. (2007) 'Abduction and Chance Discovery in Science', *International Journal of Knowledge-Based and Intelligent Engineering Systems* 11(5): 273–279.

Marmot, M. and Wilkinson, R.G. (2001) 'Psychosocial and Material Pathways in the Relation Between Income and Health: A Response to Lynch et al', *British Medical Journal* 322: 1233–1236.

Marmot, M., Ryff, C.D., Bumpass, L.L., Shipley, M. and Marks, N.F. (1997) 'Social Inequalities in Health: Next Questions and Converging Evidence', *Social Science and Medicine* 44(6): 901–910.

Marmot, M., Shipley, M.J. and Rose, G. (1984) 'Inequalities in Death: Specific Explanations of a General Pattern?', *Lancet* 323(8384): 1003–1006.

Marmot, M., Davey Smith, G., Stansfeld, S., Patel, C., North, F., Head, J., White, I., Brunner, E. and Feeney A. (1991) 'Health Inequalities among British Civil Servants: The Whitehall II Study', *Lancet* 337(8754): 1387–1393.

Marmot, M., Seigrist, J., Theorell, T. and Feeney, A. (1999) 'Health and the Psychosocial Environment at Work', in M. Marmot and R.G. Wilkinson (eds) *Social Determinants of Health.* Oxford: Oxford University Press, pp 97–130.

Marshall, T.H. (1981) *The Right to Welfare.* London: Free Press.

Martikainen, P., Stansfeld, S., Hemingway, H. and Marmot, M. (1999) 'Determinants of Socioeconomic Differences in Physical and Mental Functioning', *Social Science and Medicine* 49(4): 499–507.

Marx, K. (1977) *Economic and Philosophic Manuscripts of 1844.* London: Lawrence and Wishart.

Marx, K. (1990) *Capital Volume I.* London: Penguin Classics.

Marx, K. (1991) *Capital Volume III.* London: Penguin Classics.

Marx, K. (1993) *Grundrisse: Foundations of the Critique of Political Economy.* London: Penguin.

Marx, K. and Engels, F. (1974) *The German Ideology.* London: Lawrence and Wishart.

Marx, K. and Engels, F. (1976) *Collected Works.* London: Lawrence and Wishart.

Marx, K. and Engels, F. (1998) *The Communist Manifesto.* Oxford: Oxford University Press.

Marx, K. and Engels. F. (2015) *The Communist Manifesto.* London: Penguin Classics.

Mayer, J. and Timms, N. (1970) *The Client Speaks.* London: Routledge.

McEwan, B.S. (2000) 'Allostasis and Allostatic Load: Implications for Neuropsychopharmacology', *Neuropsychopharmacology* 22: 108–124.

McGarvey, D. (2023) *The Social Distance Between Us: How Remote Politics Wrecked Britain.* London: Penguin.

McLennan, G. (1996) 'Post-Marxism and the "'Four Sins" of Modernist Theorizing', *New Left Review* 218(218): 53–74.

Medvedyuk, S., Govender, P. and Raphael, D. (2021) 'The Reemergence of Engels' Concept of Social Murder in Response to Growing Social and Health Inequalities', *Social Science & Medicine* 289: 114377.

Meikle, S. (1985) *Essentialism in the Thought of Karl Marx*. LaSalle: Open Court.

Merle-Ponty, M. (2002) *The Phenomenology of Perception*. London: Routledge

Merrifield, A. (1999) 'Notes on Suffering and Freedom: A Marxian and Dostoevskian Encounter', *Rethinking Marxism* 11(1): 72–86.

Mészáros, I. (1975) *Marx's Theory of Alienation* (4th edition). London: Merlin Press.

Meyer, S.B. and Lunnay, B. (2012) 'The Application of Abductive and Retroductive Inference for the Design and Analysis of Theory-driven Sociological Research', *Sociological Research Online* 18(1): 12.

Miller, G.A. (1967) 'Professionals in Bureaucracy: Alienation among Industrial Scientists and Engineers', *American Sociological Review* 32(5): 755–768.

Milne, S. (2014) *The Enemy Within: The Secret War against the Miners*. London: Verso.

Mirowski, P. (2013) *Never Let a Serious Crisis Go to Waste: How Neoliberalism Survived the Financial Meltdown*. London: Verso.

Montgomery, C.A., Wernerfelt, B. and Balakrishnan, S. (1989) 'Strategy Content and the Research Process: A Critique and Commentary', *Strategic Management Journal* 10(20): 189–197.

Moore, J.W. (2016) *Anthropocene or Capitalocene? Nature, History, and the Crisis of Capitalism*. Binghamton: PM Press.

Munro, E. (2004) 'The Impact of Audit on Social Work Practice', *British Journal of Social Work* 34(8): 1073–1074.

Munro, E. (2011) *The Munro Review of Child Protection: Final Report, a Child-Centred System*. London: The Stationery Office.

Muntaner, C., Lynch, J., Hillemeier, M., J Hee Lee, J., David, R., Benach, J. and Borrell, C. (2002) 'Economic Inequality, Working-class Power, Social Capital, and Cause-specific Mortality in Wealthy Countries', *International Journal of Health Services* 32(4): 629–656.

Musto, M. (2010) 'Revisiting Marx's Concept of Alienation', *Socialism and Democracy* 24(3): 79–101.

Musto, M. (2021) *Karl Marx's Writings on Alienation*. Cham: Palgrave Macmillan.

Navarro, V. (1978) *Class Struggle, the State and Medicine: An Historical and Contemporary Analysis of the Medical Sector in Great Britain*. Oxford: Martin Robertson.

Nazroo, J.Y., Bhui, K.S. and Rhodes, J. (2020) 'Where Next for Understanding Race/Ethnic Inequalities in Severe Mental Illness? Structural, Interpersonal and Institutional Racism', *Sociology of Health & Illness* 42(2): 262–276.

Neal, A.G. and Seeman, M. (1964) 'Organizations and Powerlessness: A Test of the Mediation Hypothesis', *American Sociological Review* 29(2): 216–226.

Nielsen, C.R. (2013) 'Frantz Fanon and the Négritude Movement: How Strategic Essentialism Subverts Manichean Binaries', *Callaloo* 36(2): 342–352.

Nussbaum, M.C. (1992) 'Human Functioning and Social Justice: In Defense of Aristotelian Essentialism', *Political Theory* 20(2): 202–246.

Nussbaum, M.C. (1993) 'Human Behavior and Social Justice: On Defense of Aristotelian Essentialism', *Gemeinschaft und Gerechtigkeit*: 323–361.

Nussbaum, M.C. (1997) 'Capabilities and Human Rights', *Fordham Law Review* 66: 273–300.

Nussbaum, M.C. (2000) *Women and Human Development: The Capabilities Approach*. Cambridge: Cambridge University Press.

Nussbaum, M.C. (2006) *Frontiers of Justice: Disability, Nationality, Species Membership*. Cambridge, MA: Harvard University Press.

O'Boyle, B. and McDonough, T. (2016) 'Critical Realism and the Althusserian Legacy', *Journal for the Theory of Social Behaviour* 46(2): 143–164.

Ollman, B. (1976) *Alienation: Marx's Conception Of Man In Capitalist Society* (2nd edition). Cambridge: Cambridge University Press.

Ollman, B. (2003) *Dance of the Dialectic: Steps in Marx's Method*. Champaign: University of Illinois Press.

Orwell, G. (1946) 'Why I Write', *Gangrel* 4.

Oswald, A.J. (1997) 'Happiness and Economic Performance', *Economic Journal* 107(445): 1815–1831.

Øversveen, E. (2022) 'Capitalism and Alienation: Towards a Marxist Theory of Alienation for the 21st Century', *European Journal of Social Theory* 25(3): 440–457.

Panteli, N., Rapti, A. and Scholarios, D. (2020) '"If he just knew who we were": Microworkers' Emerging Bonds of Attachment in a Fragmented Employment Relationship', *Work, Employment and Society* 34(3): 476–494.

Parker, I. (2007) *Revolution in Psychology: Alienation to Emancipation*. London: Pluto Books.

Parsloe, P. and Stevenson, O. (1978) *Social Services Teams: The Practitioners' View*. London: HMSO.

Parsons, J.A., Eakin, J.M., Bell, R.S., Franche, R.L. and Davis, A.M. (2008) '"So, are you back to work yet?": Re-conceptualizing "Work" and "Return to Work" in the Context of Primary Bone Cancer', *Social Science & Medicine* 67(11): 1826–1836.

Pearlin, L.L. (1962) 'Alienation from Work: A Study of Personnel', *American Sociological Review* 27(3): 314–326.

Peirce, C.S. (1992) *The Essential Peirce*. Indiana: Indiana University Press.

Pettinger, L. (2019) *What's Wrong with Work?* Bristol: Policy Press.

Pirie, I. (2016) 'Disordered Eating and the Contradictions of Neoliberal Governance', *Sociology of Health & Illness* 38(6): 839–853.

Pösö, T. and Eronen, T. (2015) 'Five Years in Care: Documented Lives and Time Trajectories in Child Welfare', *Child & Family Social Work*, 20(2): 202–210.

Pritlove, C, Parissa, S., Angus. J.E., Armstrong, P., Jones, J.M. and Parsons, J. (2019) '"It's Hard Work": A Feminist Political Economy Approach to Reconceptualizing "Work" in the Cancer Context', *Qualitative Health Research* 29(5): 758–773.

Rabaka, R. (2009) *Africana Critical Theory: Reconstructing the Black Radical Tradition, from WEB Du Bois and CLR James to Frantz Fanon and Amilcar Cabral*. Plymouth: Lexington Books.

Rabaka, R. (2011) 'Revolutionary Fanonism: On Frantz Fanon's Modification of Marxism and Decolonization of Democratic Socialism', *Socialism and Democracy* 25(1): 126–145.

Ramble, P. (1979) Unknown Treasures. *New Musical Express*, 11 August.

Rand, A. (1943) *The Fountainhead*. Indianapolis: Bobbs Merrill.

Rand, A. (1957) *Atlas Shrugged*. New York: Random House.

Reed, J. (2016) *The Politics of Transindividuality: Historical Materialism*, Vol. 106. Chicago: Haymarket Books.

Rees, J. (1998) *The Algebra of Revolution: The Dialectic and the Classical Marxist Tradition*. London: Routledge.

Reichle, L.R. and Bescherer, P. (2021) 'Organizing with Tenants and Fighting Rightist Resentments', *Radical Housing Journal* 3(1): 11–31.

Renwick, D. (2009) 'The Origins of Employee Wellbeing in Brazil: An Exploratory Analysis', *Employee Relations* 31(3): 312–321.

Reuten, G.A. (1997) The Notion of Tendency in Marx's 1894 Law of Profit. In M. Campbell and F. Moseley (eds) *New Investigations of Marx's Method*. New York: Humanities Press, pp 150–175.

Reuten, G.A. (2004) '"Zirkel vicieux" or Trend Fall? The Course of the Profit Rate in Marx's Capital III', *History of Political Economy* 36(1): 163–186.

Reuten, G.A. (2014) *An Outline of the Systematic-Dialectical Method: Scientific and Political Significance of Marx's Capital and Hegel's Logic*. Leiden: Brill, pp 241–268.

Ricoeur, P. (1968) *Aliénation*. Encyclopædia universalis.

Roberts, M. and Carchedi, G. (2022) *Capitalism in the 21st Century*. London: Pluto Press.

Rosdolsky, R (1992) *The Making of Marx's Capital*, Vol. 2. London: Pluto Press.

Rose, S. (2006) *The 21st Century Brain: Explaining, Mending and Manipulating the Mind*. London: Vintage.

Rousseau, J.J. (1754) *Discourse on the Origin and Basis of Inequality Among Men*. Kindle Download.

Rousseau, J.J. (1762) *The Social Contract*. Kindle Download.

Rubenhold, H. (2019) *The Five: The Untold Lives of the Women Killed by Jack the Ripper*. London: Doubleday.

Ruskin, J. (2012) *Selections from the Works of John Ruskin*. Kindle Download.

Ryan, R.M. and Deci, E.L. (2001) 'On Happiness and Human Potentials: A Review of Research on Hedonic and Eudaimonic Well-being', *Annual Review of Psychology* 52: 141–166.

Saito, K. (2017) *Karl Marx's Ecosocialism*. New York: Monthly Review Press.

Saito, K. (2023) *Marx in the Anthropocene: Towards the Idea of Degrowth Communism*. Cambridge: Cambridge University Press.

Sapolsky, R.M. (2004) *Why Zebras Don't Get Ulcers*. London: St Martin's Press.

Sapolsky, R.M. (2018) *Behave: The Biology of Humans at Our Best and Worst*. London: Vintage.

Sayer, A. (2000) *Realism and Social Science*. London: SAGE.

Sayers, S. (1998) *Marxism and Human Nature*. London: Routledge.

Sayers, S. (2007) 'The Concept of Labor: Marx and His Critics', *Science and Society* 71(4): 431–454.

Sayers, S. (2013) *Marx and Alienation: Essays on Hegelian Themes*. London: Palgrave Macmillan.

Schilling, C. (2012) *The Body and Social Theory* (3rd edition). London: SAGE.

Schmidt, A. (1970) *The Concept of Nature in Marx*. London: New Left Books.

Seeman, M. (1959) 'On the Meaning of Alienation', *American Sociological Review* 24(6): 783–791.

Seeman, M. (1967) 'On the Personal Consequences of Alienation in Work', *American Sociological Review* 32(2): 273–285.

Seligman, M.E.P. (2002) *Authentic Happiness: Using the New Positive Psychology to Realize Your Potential for Lasting Fulfillment*. New York: Free Press.

Seligman, M.E.P. (2008) 'Positive Health', *Applied Psychology: An International Review* 57: 3–18.

Seligman, M.E.P. and Csikszentmihalyi, M. (2000) 'Positive Psychology', *American Psychologist* 55(1): 5–14.

Sennett, R. (2008) *The Craftsman*. New Haven: Yale University Press.

Sennet, R. and Cobb, J. (1972) *The Hidden Injuries of Class*. New York: Vintage Books.

Sève, L. (1978) *Man in Marxist Theory and the Psychology of Personality*. Brighton: Harvester Press.

Shepard, J.M. (1970) 'Functional Specialization, Alienation and Job Satisfaction', *Industrial and Labor Relations Review* 23(2): 207–219.

Slatman, J. (2014) *Our Strange Body*. Amsterdam: Amsterdam University Press.

Sointu, E. (2005) 'The Rise of an Ideal: Tracing Changing Discourses of Wellbeing', *The Sociological Review* 53(2): 255–274.

Spinoza, B. (1996) *Ethics*. London: Penguin.

Spivak, G. (1988) 'Can the Subaltern Speak?' In L. Grossberg and C. Nelson (eds) *Marxism and the Interpretation of Culture*. Houndmills: Macmillan, pp 66–111.

Standing, G. (2011) *The Precariat*. London: Bloomsbury.

Stanton, R.R. (2021) 'WDAS's Problematic Portrayal of Food Farming', in R.R. Stanton (ed) *The Disneyfication of Animals*. Cham: Springer International Publishing, pp 1–27.

Steger, M.F., Kashdan, T.B., Sullivan, B.A. and Lorentz, D. (2008) 'Understanding the Search for Meaning in Life: Personality, Cognitive Style, and the Dynamic Between Seeking and Experiencing Meaning', *Journal of Personality* 76(2): 199–228.

Stone C.J. (1996) *Fierce Dancing: Adventures in the Underground*. London: Faber & Faber.

Strangleman, T. (2005) 'Sociological Futures and the Sociology of Work', *Sociological Research Online* 10(4). http://www.socresonline.org.uk/10/4/strangleman.ht

Streeck, W. (2016) *How Will Capitalism End? Essays on a Failing System*. London: Verso.

Stuart, D., Schewe, R.L. and Gunderson, R. (2013) 'Extending Social Theory to Farm Animals: Addressing Alienation in the Dairy Sector', *Sociologia Ruralis* 53(2): 201–222.

Stufflebeam, D.L. and Shinkfield, A.J. (2007) *Evaluation Theory, Models, & Applications*. San Francisco: Jossey-Bass.

Tenhouten, W. (2017) *Alienation and Affect*. London: Routledge.

Thier, H. (2020) *A People's Guide to Capitalism*. Chicago: Haymarket Books.

Tooze, A. (2017) 'A General Logic of Crisis', *London Review of Books* 39(1): 3–8.

Toscano, A. (2022) '"Everything can be made better, except man": On Frédéric Lordon's Communist Realism', *Radical Philosophy* 212: 19–34.

Tsui, M.S. and Cheung, F.C.H. (2004) 'Gone with the Wind: The Impacts of Managerialism on Human Services', *The British Journal of Social Work* 34(3): 437–442.

Vidon, E.S. (2019) 'Why Wilderness? Alienation, Authenticity, and Nature', *Tourist Studies* 19(1): 3–22.

Vogel, L. (2013) *Marxism and the Oppression of Women: Toward a Unitary Theory*. Leiden: Brill.

Völker, S. and Kistemann, T. (2011) 'The Impact of Blue Space on Human Health and Well-being: Salutogenetic Health Effects of Inland Surface Waters: A Review', *International Journal of Hygiene and Environmental Health* 214(6): 449–460.

Volpato, C., Andrighetto, L. and Baldissarri, C. (2017) 'Perceptions of Low-Status Workers and the Maintenance of the Social Class Status Quo', *Journal of Social Issues* 73(1): 192–210.

Wainwright, D. and Calnan, M. (2002) *Work Stress: The Making of a Modern Epidemic*. Buckingham: Open University Press.

Wainwright, D. and Calnan, M. (2011) 'The Fall of Work Stress and the Rise of Wellbeing', in S. Vickerstaff, C. Phillipson and R. Wilkie (eds) *Work, Health and Wellbeing: The Challenges of Managing Health at Work*. Bristol: Policy Press, pp 161–186.

Waite, L. (2006) *Embodied Working Lives*. Lanham: Lexington Books.

Walsh, Z. (2016) 'A Meta-Critique of Mindfulness Critiques: From McMindfulness to Critical Mindfulness', in R. Purser, D. Forbes and A. Burke (eds) *Handbook of Mindfulness: Mindfulness in Behavioral Health*. Cham: Springer.

Wang, N. (1999) 'Rethinking Authenticity in Tourism Experience', *Annals of Tourism Research* 26(2): 349–370.

Waylen, G. (1997) 'Gender, Feminism and Political Economy', *New Political Economy* 2(2): 205–220.

Webster, J. (2016) 'Microworkers of the Gig Economy: Separate and Precarious', *New Labor Forum* 25(3): 56–64.

Wendling, A. (2011) *Karl Marx on Technology and Alienation*. London: Palgrave Macmillan.

Wilde, L. (2000) '"The Creatures, Too, Must Become Free": Marx and the Animal/Human Distinction', *Capital & Class* 24(3): 37–53.

Wilde, L. (2011) 'Marx, Morality, and the Global Justice Debate', *Global Discourse* 2(1): 24–38.

Wilkinson, I. (2004) *Suffering: A Sociological Introduction*. London: Polity Press.

Wilkinson, R.G. (1996) *Unhealthy Societies: The Afflictions of Inequality*. London: Routledge.

Wilkinson, R.G. and Pickett, K.E. (2006) 'Income Inequality and Population Health: A Review and Explanation of the Evidence', *Social Science and Medicine* 62(7): 1768–1784.

Wilkinson, R.G. and Pickett, K. (2010) *The Spirit Level: Why Equality is Better for Everyone*. London: Penguin.

Wilkinson, R.G. and Pickett, K. (2019) *The Inner Level: How More Equal Societies Reduce Stress, Restore Sanity and Improve Everyone's Well-being*. London: Penguin.

Williams, C. (2010) 'Affective Processes without a Subject: Rethinking the Relation Between Subjectivity and Affect with Spinoza', *Subjectivity* 3: 245–262.

Williams, C. (2017) 'Unravelling the Subject with Spinoza: Towards a Morphological Analysis of the Scene of Subjectivity', *Contemporary Political Theory* 16: 342–362.

Williams, D.R. and Mohammed, S.A. (2013) 'Racism and Health I: Pathways and Scientific Evidence', *The American Behavioral Scientist* 57(8).

Williams, D.R., Lawrence, J.A. and Davis, B.A. (2019) 'Racism and Health: Evidence and Needed Research', *Annual Review of Public Health* 40(1): 105–125.

Williams, J.M.G. and Kuyken, W. (2012) 'Mindfulness-based Cognitive Therapy: A Promising New Approach to Preventing Depressive Relapse', *British Journal of Psychiatry* 200(5): 359–360.

Williams, O. and Annandale, E. (2020) 'Obesity, Stigma and Reflexive Embodiment: Feeling the "Weight" of Expectation', *Health* 24(4): 421–441.

Williams, R. (1976) *Keywords: A Vocabulary of Culture and Society*. London: Verso.

Williams, S.J. (1998) 'Modernity and the Emotions: Corporeal Reflections on the (Ir)rational', *Sociology* 32(4): 747–769.

Williams, S.J. (2000) *Emotion and Social Theory: Corporeal Reflections on the (Ir)rational*. London: SAGE.

Williams, S.J. (2003a) 'Beyond Meaning Discourse and the Empirical World', *Social Theory and Health* 1(1): 42–71.

Williams, S.J. (2003b) *Medicine and the Body*. London: SAGE.

Williams, S.J. (2006) 'Medical Sociology and the Biological Body: Where Are We Now and Where Do We Go from Here?', *Health* 10(1): 5–30.

Wood, A.W. (2004) *Karl Marx*. Abingdon: Routledge.

World Health Organization (2020) 'The Global Health Observatory'. https://www.who.int/data/gho/data/themes/mortality-and-global-health-estimates/ghe-life-expectancy-and-healthy-life-expectancy

Xue, L., Manuel-Navarrete, D. and Buzinde, C.N. (2014) 'Theorizing the Concept of Alienation in Tourism Studies', *Annals of Tourism Research* 44: 186–199.

Yuill, C. (2005) 'Marx: Capitalism, Alienation and Health', *Social Theory and Health* 3: 126–143.

Yuill, C. (2010) '"The Spirit Level", Health Inequalities and Economic Democracy', *International Journal of Management Concepts and Philosophy* 4(2): 177–193.

Yuill, C. (2011) 'Forgetting and Remembering Alienation', *The History of Human Sciences* 24(2): 103–119.

Yuill, C. (2017) 'The Use of Abduction in Alienation Research: A Rationale and a Worked Example', *Social Theory & Health*, 15: 465–481.

Yuill, C. (2018) 'Social Workers and Alienation: The Compassionate Self and the Disappointed Juggler', *Critical and Radical Social Work* 6(3): 275–289.

Yuill, C. (2021) 'The Fleeting Solidarities of the Pandemic?', *Cost of Living*. https://www.cost-ofliving.net/the-fleeting-solidarities-of-the-pandemic/

Zahar, R. (1974) *Frantz Fanon: Colonialism and Alienation*. New York: New York University Press.

Zak, P.J., Kurzban, R. and Matzner, W.T. (2005) 'Oxytocin is Associated with Human Trustworthiness', *Hormones and Behavior* 48(5): 522–527.

Zak, P.J., Stanton, A.A. and Ahmadi, S. (2007) 'Oxytocin Increases Generosity in Humans', *PLOS ONE* 2(11): e1128.

Zelený, J. (1980) *The Logic of Marx*. Oxford: Blackwell.

Žižek, S. (2008) *Violence*. London: Profile Books.

Žižek, Z. (2009) *First as Tragedy, Then as Farce*. London: Verso.

Zoubir, Z. (2018) '"Alienation" and Critique in Marx's Manuscripts of 1857–58 ("Grundrisse")', *The European Journal of the History of Economic Thought* 25(5): 710–737.

Index

References to endnotes show both the page number and the note number (131n5).